KEMETIC SPIRITUALITY

The Buried Secrets to Spiritual Evolution, the Forgotten Principles of an Elevated Existence, & the Ancient Wisdom of Divine Oneness

ASCENDING VIBRATIONS

Ascending Vibrations

AUSET

CONTENTS

CLAIM YOUR BONUSES
BELOW

To help you on your spiritual journey, we've created some free bonuses to help you clear energetic baggage that no longer serves you and manifest a life that suits you better. Bonuses include a companion video course that includes over 4.5 hours of empowering content, energy-tapping videos, powerful guided meditations, journals, and more.

You can get immediate access by going to the link below or scanning the QR code with your cell phone.

https://bonus.ascendingvibrations.net

Free Bonus #1: The 3-Step Chakra Tune-Up Course

Want to know a unique way to target the chakras? Elevate Your Existence by Targeting the Subconscious, the Physical, & the Spiritual

- Discover a unique 3-step chakra targeting method that so many people aren't taking advantage of!
- Hack your brain, elevate body, mind, and spirit, and release blocks holding you back from greatness
- Awaken amazing energy to tailor a reality that suits you better
- Stop wasting precious time on ineffective methods

Free Bonus #2: The Manifesting Secret Formula Toolkit

Are you done with settling in life, wasting precious time, and ready to attract your highest potential to you?

Free Bonus #3: The Spiritual Cleansing Toolkit

Are you ready to drop all of the negative energy that no longer serves you?

- Release energetic blocks that could be causing imbalances
- Awaken amazing energy to supercharge your aura
- Create a beautifully cleansed, energetic environment

Free Bonus #4: A Powerful 10-Minute Energy Healing Guided Meditation

All of these amazing bonuses are 100% free. You don't need to enter any details except for your email address.

To get instant access to your bonuses, go to

https://bonus.ascendingvibrations.net

RA

INTRODUCTION

KEMETIC SPIRITUALITY CAN ELECTRIFY YOUR SPIRITUAL PRACTICE TODAY

Nature or Ntr is the ultimate divine force. This is what Kemetic spirituality, a way of life that emanated from ancient Egypt, also known as Kemet, tells us. It provides a set of guidelines and practices to live by that are based on the ancient ways of living. People are increasingly turning to this way of life as a means of maintaining a balanced lifestyle amid the chaos of modern-day living. This Kemetic way of life that is being discovered by an increasing number of people encourages us to live in alignment with nature. This is accomplished through self-awareness. Practicing this self-awareness involves many techniques, such as meditation and yoga. It also requires an understanding of the impact that your diet has on your body. Such knowledge provides you with the direction to make better food choices for spiritual growth. The long-term result of these improved choices is a longer life and a disease-free body. If you have incorporated yoga and meditation into your lifestyle, this longer life can be an enjoyable one.

Living a long and enjoyable lifestyle is possible when guided by Kemetic spirituality, as it encourages you to receive guidance from the divine forces of nature. This guidance is embodied in the Metu Neter, the writings found on temple walls and papyruses that contain teachings from nature. The Metu Neter is also known as the word of the gods. Its teachings explain the relationship between humanity and the divine. They define human spirituality in relation to our alignment with the principles of the gods and goddesses—the Neter.

These gods and goddesses embody the physical and spiritual principles of creation. The relationship between these principles of creation finds their full expression in the Kemetic tree of life.

The words of the Metu Neter that are recorded on the walls of temples and papyruses are the oldest recorded spiritual system known to man. By studying these words, we learn about the connection between mankind and the gods and goddesses of ancient Egypt, also known as Kemet. When we apply them in our lives, we learn how to live in a way that highlights the divine spirit within us.

Modern spiritual exploration, with the discovery of concepts such as atomic science and the knowledge of Hermetic laws, has come to embrace concepts such as vibration. These are concepts that were well-known and put into practice by those who lived during Kemetic times and upon which Kemetic spirituality is based. With the knowledge of spiritual balance and the continuous uplifting of their mental vibration, inhabitants of ancient Kemet established a prosperous society that was well-educated. Their high level of knowledge resulted in them accomplishing great scientific and architectural feats that we are still able to admire today. By following in their footsteps and emulating their way of life, you will be able to live at a level where your mind, body, and soul are in alignment with the divine. This will enable you to enjoy a productive and positive life without the distractions that emanate from a low vibrational existence. Instead, Kemetic spirituality encourages us to live in positive vibrational alignment daily.

Kemetic spirituality encourages us to be constantly aware that there is interconnectedness between humanity and the divine. That the world around us is an extension of who we are. It teaches us that there is divinity in the most basic forms of human existence. Yet because divinity exists on different planes of existence, we can choose to align within divinity at different levels. The higher the levels or planes of existence that we align with, the closer we become to god. This pursuit of the embodiment of godliness, of wanting to be like the gods and goddesses, is known as theurgy.

The practice of theurgy requires knowledge of the Kemetic creation story. This story explains how creation came into existence and how with each step in the creation process, a different principle or force of nature came into existence. Each force existed to fulfill the purpose that was needed at that time. The principles that were thus employed in the creation process became the gods and goddesses that we now see evidence of on temple walls and on the scrolls of papyrus scripts. Therefore, at the core of Kemetic spirituality lies an understanding of the gods and goddesses, the principles they embody, their behavior, and even the poses that they stand or sit in at the various places where they are depicted. Knowledge of all of these will give you the knowledge and insight that you need to implement the principles that these gods and goddesses symbolize.

THE CREATION STORY

The creation story starts with Ra. He is the sun god and the source of life and sustenance for all living things. In the creation story, we see Ra emerging from the primeval waters of Nun. Before Ra emerges, the waters of Nun are the only thing on earth. These chaotic waters cover everything in sight. In creating the world, Ra starts with the causal plane that includes the structures that govern the world. These structures are the laws of science that maintain balance and order and thus provide an environment that allows all things to exist. This balance and order is represented by the goddess Ma'at who enables harmony to exist in the world.

After the spiritual laws, Ra then created the atmosphere. This is what allows all living creatures to exist. The atmosphere consists of dry air mixed with water. The dry air is what we breathe. It is also the ethereal and is represented by the god Shu. Shu is the god of the air, the one that separates the earth and the sky. Contained within the dry air of Shu is the precipitation that forms rain, snow, and hail. This is represented by the goddess Tefnut, the goddess of moisture. Thus, the earth was filled with a gaseous substance or a mist.

Shu and Tefnut came together and formed heaven and earth, which they hold separate from each other by coming in between them. The heavenly skies that contain the stars are depicted by the goddess Nut, who stretches out with her limbs touching down on either side of the earth. Nut, the goddess of the sky, is often depicted with the stars of the milky way painted on her body to demonstrate her celestial nature. Nut swallows the sun god—also known as Ra—every evening and gives birth to him in the morning. This gives us sunrise and sunset. When Ra, the sun god, is in a state of rising, he is referred to as Ra-Khepri. His state at sunset is referred to as Ra-Atum. The earth is represented by the god Geb, and he is the ground that lies stretched out below the overarching Nut.

Once the earth had been formed, human beings were created. In our complexity as humans, we have different aspects that make up who we are. One of these aspects is the ego, which we temper through the application of wisdom and intuition. The ego within humanity is represented by the god Set, and wisdom and intuition are represented by the god Aset. These aspects of the human personality are made possible because mankind is an eternal soul. The eternal soul is represented by the god Asar. In Greek mythology, Asar is known as Osiris, the god whose brother Seth cuts up into 14 pieces out of jealousy.

These are the elements that Ra created, alongside the two goddesses of creation in the form of the principles Nebethetepet and Iusaaset. These goddesses, respectively, are co-creator with Ra and the grandmother to the gods. Together, the three form a divine triangle that creates the tree of life.

When the Kemetic creation story is told, it does not use the names of principles and elements like 'balance' and 'order' or 'air' and 'water.' Rather, it is personalized, and these elements and principles are given names of gods and goddesses. To align with this method of storytelling, cast your mind back to kindergarten drama class. Imagine an end-of-year concert whereby every single child is given a unique role to play. No matter how minor it is, that role requires a special costume that is created for display. The play is an opportunity for the child's acting and showcasing of their costume for their proud parents. Sometimes that role is as innocuous as "a tree blowing in the wind." Yet it gives the child a sense of participation as they fully embrace the role or element with which they have been entrusted. When you practice theurgy, you behave in the same way as these children at the school play. You totally become the principle whose properties you have decided to adopt. This means understanding the god or goddess that is embodied by that principle. In so doing, seek to find out their background story and the challenges that they underwent. Find out the part that they played in the creation story and the element that they embody. In understanding this, you will be better equipped to face challenges in your life. You can align yourself with the principle that best enables you to overcome the challenges that you are facing. The principle that already overcame your challenges can be called upon to help you overcome your present challenges. You can emulate their attitude and behavior. You thus practice theurgy by becoming the principle that has overcome the challenges and transcended to the next plane of existence.

So, if you are that tree blowing in the wind, what sound do you make? What actions do you engage in? What is the experience of anybody who interacts with you? If we expand that analogy a bit further to elements such as air, water, and heat, we then step into the world of ancient Kemet and the gods and goddesses that make up the creation story.

For in that creation story, we have elements that appeared in the same order that their virtues were needed. These elements, which take on the names of gods and goddesses, are the following:

- Djehuti (The god of the moon)
- Ma'at (The goddess of balance and harmony)
- Het-Heru (Hathor, the beautiful goddess of festivities)
- Shu (The god of the air)
- Tefnut (Goddess of moisture and precipitation)
- Nut (Goddess of the night sky)
- Geb (God of the earth)
- Asar (God of vegetation)
- Set (God of chaos, confusion, destruction, storms, foreign lands, eclipses, earthquakes, and violence)
- Aset (Goddess of wisdom and intuition)
- Nebthet (Goddess of the air)
- Heru Ur (God of war and the sky)
- Nbt hotep (Nebethetepet, or Nbt hotep, represents rest. Alongside motion, which is

represented by Iusaaset, they create time and space. Thus, these two come together with Ra to form a triangle that is the foundation of time and space. This foundation enables Ra to create the world)

- Iusaaset (Grandmother of the gods and goddesses)

We also need to understand the creation story as it provides a pathway to follow when we are seeking enlightenment. An understanding of the process of creation will make you aware of the principles that were active at the time and that you must employ if you want to raise your vibration to an energetic level that brings you closer to alignment with the divine.

Although the meaning of the word Kemet means "land of the blacks" or "the black land," we should understand that prior to such a name being used, the spirituality that was practiced in that land existed for more than 3,000 years. When we compare this to the fact that the first migration of mankind from Africa to Asia and onwards to the rest of the globe occurred between 80,000 to 15,000 years ago, and has continued ever since, we come to realize why traces of Kemetic spirituality are evident in the religious practices of people everywhere. Scholars used to travel from across the globe to learn the wisdom and spirituality of ancient Egypt before returning to their own countries and adapting it to their local cultures. Traces of this ancient wisdom and spirituality can be found interlaced with local beliefs throughout the world. Therefore, by embracing Kemetic spirituality, you are embracing beliefs that mankind has held onto for thousands of years and which are still practiced for their relevance to our lives today. Discoveries made by modern science, such as knowledge of atoms and holograms, have resulted in a more enlightened outlook regarding the human mind and its capabilities. Books such as *Quantum Warrior* By John Kehoe go into detail on the connection between atoms, vibration, and the human mind. He argues that through the use of affirmations, you can align yourself with the quantum field using the power of vibration. In doing this, we manifest the lives we want to live (Kehoe, 2011). As you go through the pages of this book, you will realize that these are just some of the concepts that are embodied in the practices of ancient Kemet.

The Kemetic spiritual walk is more than a religion; it is a way of life. Rather than focus on a single aspect, such as prayer, meditation, or diet, as a means of aligning oneself with the divine, Kemetic spirituality engages all these aspects. Indeed, it embraces all aspects of your life and informs the way in which you conduct your daily activities, from the moment you wake up to the time you retire to bed.

For this reason, it is beneficial to understand that there is an interconnectedness between each chapter of this book. The chapters may be set out individually, which provides you with the ability to review individual concepts alone. However, it helps to understand that each chapter and each discipline is interlinked. Divinity runs throughout our lives and their processes in the same way that all principles and forces that were employed in the creation of the world came from a single divine force. You cannot separate yourself from divinity, and to purposefully live in alignment with the divine is to achieve success in multiple areas of your life.

Set

❧ I ❧

HOW TO BEGIN PRACTICING KEMETIC SPIRITUALITY AND WHAT YOU MUST UNDERSTAND FOR ACCELERATED SPIRITUAL GROWTH

To begin your practice of Kemetic spirituality, you must understand that the world was created out of Nun. Nun is the nothingness that existed before spirit, in the form of Ra, who rose from it and gradually formed the world. Creation itself occurred in such a way that higher states of consciousness were created before lower states of vibration existed. With each form of consciousness that was created, a lower form of consciousness was born from it. This occurred until physical elements were manifested in the form of the earth and all that is on it.

Humanity, a solid form, is bound to the effects of the ego and, thus, exists in a low vibrational state. Spiritual practice aims to lift humanity from the lower vibrational awareness to a position whereby one lives daily in alignment with God, able to call creations into existence the same way that God did during the process of creation.

Alignment with God is achieved by maintaining a state of balance. This state of balance is extremely important in the practice of Kemetic spirituality. The goddess Ma'at, who embodies this balance, influences the daily life of the Kemetic up to and beyond the state of death. Alignment with God can also be brought about by following daily practices that keep you mindful of what you feed your body, mind, and spirit. Each activity that you undertake in the nourishment of these areas of your life should work to bring you closer to your own state of godliness.

ACHIEVING BALANCE

Kemetic spirituality is based on the balance of spiritual law and order in the lives of those who practice it. Once balance is lost from your own life, you will find it difficult to align with source. The divine source brings about order, whereas a state of disorder is one in which potential still has to be realized, much like the waters of Nun before creation began.

To achieve a state of balance, we must be aware of the activities and teachings of the goddess Ma'at. To ensure that balance was maintained, initiates studied the 42 laws of Ma'at, the goddess who embodies the laws of balance and harmony. Ma'at is she who weighs the heart or spirit of each initiate as it passes through the halls of judgment after death. This is done to determine whether they are worthy of passing through to the afterlife.

The Kemetites believed that when a person died, their

heart would be weighed by Ma'at against the feather of truth. She is depicted with this ostrich feather in all her illustrations. The feather was what she used to weigh a person's heart after death to determine whether the person could embark on their journey into the afterlife. Those who failed the test would end their journey within the Hall of Judgment, where they would get consumed by Ammu—a cross between a crocodile, a hippopotamus, and a lion. This consumption would be a final death for that soul, and they would not experience the afterlife, nor would they experience a reincarnated life on earth.

To ensure that one's journey was not prematurely halted, Kemetites engaged in a ritual that put the 42 laws of Ma'at at the center of their daily activities. Therefore, this would also be a good place for you to start your practice.

As a practitioner of Kemetic spirituality, you can use the 42 laws of Ma'at to guide your daily activities. This can be done by starting your day off with prayer in a form that recognizes and incorporates the laws of Ma'at. It is beneficial to do this in the morning between 4 a.m. and 6 a.m. before you continue with the activities of each day. It is best to recite these laws again at the end of the day to help you reflect on whether you were able to adequately follow through with your intentions for the day.

The Laws of Ma'at are listed below, along with a few words indicating how each law can be interpreted and applied in your life.

THE 42 LAWS OF MA'AT

1. I have not committed sin.

This refers to the absence of wrongdoing. It honors virtue in all of one's actions.

2. I have not committed robbery with violence.

This law highlights two negative actions. The first action is robbery, which deprives another person of what rightfully belongs to them. The second action is the violent nature with which this is done. The violent act disturbs a person's inner peace in addition to the disturbance caused by the loss of their belongings. Therefore, you will impact another person's ability to live in peace and harmony if you break this law.

3. I have not stolen.

The law is closely related to the previous one in that when you steal, you deprive another person of their personal belongings. You additionally cause them mental disturbance, affecting their ability to live in Ma'at.

4. I have not slain men or women.

Murder is wrong, regardless of the situation.

5. I have not stolen food.

When you steal food, you deprive another of the ability to nourish their body.

6. I have not swindled offerings.

When you make an offering to the gods and goddesses, be honest about what you are offering. Do not pretend to have offered more than you have. Do not take away from what was meant for the offering and use it for yourself, as you would then be stealing from the deities. They will know what you have done, and you may be deprived of the blessing that was meant for you or even suffer a worse fate, like eternal death in the afterworld.

7. I have not stolen from God/Goddess.

This relates to taking what has been offered to the gods and goddesses. This could have been offered by other people, or as in the previous law, could be offerings that you were supposed to make.

8. I have not told lies.

When you tell lies, you are living against the principles of Ma'at. Truth is an important aspect of living in balance and harmony; therefore, one should strive to be honest in all one says.

9. I have not carried away food.

A situation where food could be carried away can come about in a buffet situation. Some people feel justified in packing some food from the buffet to take home with them. This could be for themselves to consume later or share with those whom they did not attend with. When this is done, it could result in not enough food being available for the guests who are present at the event. Therefore, it is a very inconsiderate act, and such selfishness should be avoided.

10. I have not cursed.

To curse goes beyond uttering swear words as we know cursing to entail today. To curse somebody is to wish them ill. It is the opposite of blessing them. It is better to bless somebody than to curse them.

11. I have not closed my ears to truth.

Ma'at is the goddess of truth. Therefore, it is not enough to speak the truth; you need to also allow others to speak their truth and be heard.

12. I have not committed adultery.

Adultery is the act of sleeping with somebody else's wife or husband. This could also relate to the act of cheating on your own spouse. Do not put yourself in the position of enjoying what is not yours. You may find yourself needing to lie about your actions or needing to behave deceptively to hide what you have done.

13. I have not made anyone cry.

There are many reasons why somebody could cry as a result of your actions. This could be a deliberate attempt to harm them, a lie or an omission, or acting unkindly toward them. Act thoughtfully toward others to avoid them being saddened by your actions.

14. I have not felt sorrow without reason.

Try and live your life with joy and in accordance with your highest ideals. If you feel sad, identify the reason for it and deal with it, lest you slip into a depressive state.

15. I have not assaulted anyone.

Avoid violent behavior, especially toward others. Physical and psychological assault can have a long-term negative effect on the person being assaulted, as they could suffer from trauma as a result.

16. I am not deceitful.

Do not allow your thoughts, words, and actions to result in dishonest behavior. Act with integrity at all times.

17. I have not stolen anyone's land.

Land was important in Kemet as it was the source of food production and, thus, a means for people to sustain themselves and their families. When you apply this thinking to our modern era, make sure that you do not take away another's livelihood.

18. I have not been an eavesdropper.

You should allow people the privacy of the conversations that they engage in behind closed doors or when they believe they are alone. If you are going to listen in on a conversation, the people having the conversation should be made aware of your presence so that they can decide whether they would like to share the information with you or not.

19. I have not falsely accused anyone.

When you know that somebody has done nothing wrong, do not accuse them of doing wrong. You are lying and ruining their reputation.

20. I have not been angry without reason.

Try and avoid having a hot temper, as that can result in you becoming angry for no reason. This has a negative effect on those around you and on the way that people perceive and interact with you. Try to live and communicate in a calm manner. When you do eventually get angry, there needs to be a reason for it.

21. I have not seduced anyone's wife.

This is in alignment with the 12th law. Seducing somebody's wife can result in adultery, and this is to be avoided.

22. I have not polluted myself.

Do not partake in or consume substances that are harmful to your body. Try to keep your body pure by staying away from substances such as drugs that can cause bodily deterioration, especially to those organs known as the Children of Heru, which ensure a healthy body.

23. I have not terrorized anyone.

Do not behave in a manner that causes another to live in fear. Allow each individual to live in confidence and in peace.

24. I have not disobeyed the Law.

Follow the law of the land that has been set out by the judges and rulers of the country you live in. Also, strive to live in accordance with the Laws of Ma'at.

25. I have not been exclusively angry.

In as much as you should not be angry without reason, as stated in law 20, try not to be consumed by anger. This will cause you to continuously maintain an angry state of mind until it is eventually a part of your personality.

26. I have not cursed God/Goddess.

You should strive to live in alignment with the gods and goddesses and not curse them. You should rather seek their favor. If you feel that a god or goddess is not blessing you in accordance with your expectation, seek the reason why this may be the case rather than cursing them. Cursing them could result in a further delay in receiving some of your blessings and requested protection.

27. I have not behaved with violence.

When you act with violence, you are not acting peacefully. You should strive to maintain peace and balance at all times.

28. I have not caused disruption of peace.

This is related to the law above. Act peacefully and allow other people to act peacefully. Try to refrain from behaving in a manner that will disturb people's emotions or disrupt the peace in a neighborhood. An example of this could be playing loud music in an elderly neighborhood and thus causing most of the residents to feel irritated.

29. I have not acted hastily or without thought.

Think thoroughly about your proposed actions before you make them. In this way, you will ensure that you will not regret your actions in the future.

30. I have not overstepped my boundaries of concern.

Try not to be a busybody, concerning yourself with other people's business. Engage yourself only with those matters that concern you. This way, you will avoid falling prey to gossip and talk that is instigated by idle minds.

31. I have not exaggerated my words when speaking.

When relaying news or a story about what happened, try not to attempt to gain more attention by exaggerating the details of what took place. This can sometimes be tantamount to lying and may even cause harm to those to whom the story relates.

32. I have not worked evil.

Act with goodness and integrity always. Refrain from acting with harmful intentions, as this is evil behavior.

33. I have not used evil thoughts, words, or deeds.

This is related to the previous law and is a reminder to live with purity of word, thought, and deed.

34. I have not polluted the water.

Water gives life to every living thing. Be kind to yourself, to humanity, and to life throughout the earth by keeping the waterways clean and fresh.

35. I have not spoken angrily or arrogantly.

Do not be haughty in your behavior or in your communication. Be kind and humble in your engagements.

36. I have not cursed anyone in thought, word, or deeds.

It is best not to wish harm on anybody. Neither should you tell them that you wish them any kind of harm, especially not in a way that conveys your genuinely harmful intentions toward them. Additionally, it is best to refrain from engaging in any activity that you know will bring harm to anybody.

37. I have not placed myself on a pedestal.

It is best not to think too highly of yourself. Thinking and behaving in a humble manner is advantageous to you and everyone around you. Refrain from letting your ego drive your actions.

38. I have not stolen what belongs to a God/Goddess.

You may come across items that have been offered to a god or goddess. No matter how appealing it is to your senses, do not make these items your belongings. Leave them there for the gods or goddesses to whom they have been sacrificed. Taking them to be your own could result in a negative effect on your life.

39. I have not stolen from or disrespected the deceased.

When people were buried in Kemet, they were buried with treasures and items that were to be used in their journey to the afterlife. This law was to discourage people from becoming grave robbers. In modern times, you can implement this by respecting the wishes of the deceased when they have left a will with implicit instructions. You can also avoid taking items that have been left at a gravesite as a clear remembrance of a loved one. Respect the dead.

40. I have not taken food from a child.

Children are to be looked after and not abused. Do not take food from a child or any other things that are meant to nourish and sustain that child.

41. I have not acted with insolence.

Acting with insolence means that you have acted disrespectfully. Make sure that you treat everyone you encounter with respect. This should not be dependent on whether you believe they deserve such respect or not; it is best if you just treat them well.

42. I have not destroyed property belonging to a God/Goddess.

This is in alignment with the law numbered 38, which is a declaration of not having stolen from a god or goddess. Likewise, it is best if you look after and honor what belongs to the gods and goddesses by not destroying it.

CHILDREN OF HERU

During the mummification process, specific gods known as the Children of Heru were given the responsibility of looking after identified internal organs during the journey into the afterlife. These gods were called Hapi, Imsety, Duamutef, and Qebehsenuef, who were given the responsibility for the stomach, intestines, lungs, and liver, respectively. The identified organs were mummified and placed in canopic jars. Each jar bore the likeness of the god who guarded the body organ contained within. This preservation process highlights the importance of the body and these particular organs in this life and the next.

Therefore, it is good to recognize the importance of your body as the vessel that carries your spirit through the journey of life on earth. Part of doing this involves including blessings for the organs that were specifically charged to the Children of Heru after death. Examining each of these body parts provides insight as to why they are important for your daily life.

Hapi, the god with a baboon head, takes care of the lungs. They enable the breathing of life-giving oxygen into your body. This oxygen is needed by each cell of your body to survive. Once you are unable to breathe, you die.

The human-headed Imsety looks after your liver. The liver secretes some of the most important hormones and enzymes to enable the digestion of food. In addition to this, the liver breaks down some of the less nutritious substances we consume. This includes drugs and alcohol, which the liver breaks down so that they are not toxic to the body. The liver breaks down fats and stores glucose, making it important for our ability to thrive both in times of drought and plenty.

The jackal-headed Duamutef protects the stomach. The stomach is the first receptacle for our food once we have chewed and swallowed it. It kills off harmful substances and engages in the digestive process.

Qebehsenuef is depicted on the canopic jar with a falcon head. He looks after the intestines. The intestines enable you to absorb food into your body and consist of the small intestine and the large intestine. Each of these sections has different functions in the digestive process. The vagus nerve, which contains the brain-gut connection, runs from the intestines to the brain. Thus, any disturbance in the intestines has a direct impact on mental clarity and the way individuals can engage with and enjoy the world around them.

To aid your spiritual journey, it is advisable to strengthen your body and mind in addition to your spirit.

To strengthen your body, it is advantageous to follow a Kemetic diet. Following this diet ensures that whatever you consume provides you with positive energy emanating directly from the sun—the source of energy for the earth.

BUILDING A HEALTHY BODY

A diet containing foods that are non-organic and which are not in alignment with Kemetic principles has resulted in the unhealthy populations of modern society. This is largely due to the rise of diseases caused by consuming foods that are detrimental to our health. Some of these popular foods, such as dairy, processed foods, and seafood, result in inflammation, congestion, and the depletion of energy. The latter is due to the huge efforts required to digest these foods. These foods often give rise to allergies. Thus, instead of providing easily accessible nourishment to our bodies, these foods eventually lead to chronic illness as our bodies struggle to cope with the detrimental effects of a diet that does nothing to uplift our vibrational frequency. Instead, the wrong diet leaves us feeling bloated and lacking energy. This lack of physical energy can impact our ability to focus and pursue our spiritual path.

PHYSICAL STRENGTH AND BALANCE

Ensuring healthy bodily functions and alignment with the divine is further enhanced by the incorporation of Kemetic yoga into our daily lifestyle. Why not start your day with the breathing techniques and stretching that Kemetic yoga provides? This enables you to maintain a strong body core and incorporate the breath of life as a force that will still your mind and enable you to focus fully on your daily activities. (See the *Bonus* *Kemetic Yoga for Energizing Modern Day Practice* chapter at the end of this book.)

A meditative practice that includes an alignment with your spiritual guides also helps to build your physical body. It is through interaction with your spirit guides that you can achieve balance and healing in areas of the body that traditional western medicine either does not recognize or treats with chemicals that may not be beneficial to overall health. A spiritual approach to well-being will have a long-term positive effect on both the body and psyche.

A HEALTHY MIND

Focusing on spiritual studies will keep your mind and spirit in a realm that enables you to create positive events in your life. These spiritual studies can be taken from many of the positive religions of the world. These religions, such as Christianity, Judaism, Islam, and Buddhism, are all said to have originated in ancient Kemet. Many of the themes taught and the stories told in these religions have maintained their Kemetic origins, although names may have been changed and storylines adjusted. However, the principles that are imparted to their followers remain the same, with central themes such as the Ten Commandments being said to have been derived from the laws of Ma'at.

To maintain a healthy mind, you must also focus your mind on positive thoughts. Be mindful of thoughts that are imbued with anger, sadness, worry, and jealousy. These thoughts can result in the appearance of physical ailments over time as your body's organs begin to react to the chemicals and enzymes that are secreted into the body when such thoughts are entertained. Kemetic spirituality was aware of this connection and encouraged pure thinking thousands of years ago. It is only recently that scientific studies have recognized this correlation. If you do not take care to monitor and stabilize your negative thoughts, this could have an epigenetic effect in the long run (Mate, 2022). An epigenetic effect is one which affects you at a genetic level and thus can be passed on to your offspring. Thus, the liver disease that you brought about by too much worry could become hereditary, as both your children and grandchildren could develop it. Therefore, some types of diseases that are seen to be genetic can be avoided simply by maintaining a pureness of mind. Once you recognize that a healthy state of mind can have an effect on your overall well-being, you can work toward ensuring that your environment and your lifestyle allow this healthy mind to flourish.

To ensure that you maintain a positive outlook for most of your life, it would be beneficial to choose a profession that is in alignment with your personality (Muata Ashby, 2002). In this way, when you focus on your work, it becomes a meditative practice. If, during your work day, you are mostly in a state of ease, you will be less prone to disease. The positive emotions that stem from enjoying your work will result in a continuous positive outlook. This will have a beneficial impact on your health in both the short and long term.

THE SEVEN HERMETIC PRINCIPLES

In addition to the laws of Ma'at, the seven Hermetic Principles are a further means of achieving balance. These Hermetic principles have persisted in their application around the world. Their adoption into Greek culture has greatly influenced their ability to persist in modern-day spiritual understanding. The Hermetic Principles were given to us by the god Hermes Trismegistus. Alongside theurgy and astrology, they will enable you to access the wisdom of the universe. I will mention these principles briefly here and elaborate on them further in the chapter on Kemetic Science.

1. The Principle of Mentalism
2. The Principle of Correspondence
3. The Principle of Vibration
4. The Principle of Polarity
5. The Principle of Rhythm
6. The Principle of Causality
7. The Principle of Gender

Together, these principles should guide you on your journey as a spiritual initiate as you go about making your daily decisions.

BECOMING DIVINE

Kemetism is theurgy more than theology. What this means is that it goes beyond studying the gods and goddesses. It is a way of life where you strive to be like the gods and goddesses by embracing their positive aspects. You need to understand the challenges that the gods and goddesses faced during the course of their lives and then work toward overcoming those challenges in your own life. You can learn from the routes that were taken by the gods and goddesses and allow these to inspire you. Beyond mimicry, theurgy also involves actively calling upon the deities to be present in your life and guide your daily affairs. Doing this involves prayer, rituals, and other spiritual practices such as yoga. This enables you to use the presence and energy of the deity to assist you in getting through challenges in much the same way that wearing a raincoat allows you to walk through the rain without getting wet. The raincoat does not render you waterproof; however, it does stop you from being directly impacted by the water. When wearing a raincoat, you arrive dry at your destination. When practicing theurgy, you overcome the challenges of daily living without the deep emotional and spiritual impact that some events can bring. Practicing theurgy can also help you over-come the impact of previous negative events. This provides you with the best platform to achieve your life goals.

In addition to learning about their lives, you can work more closely with universal laws and energy. You can do this by deliberately partaking in rituals such as paying homage to your ancestors and spirit guides. It will aid you in paying attention to the Hermetic laws and living in a way that brings you in alignment with them. The ability to do this and thus manipulate events in their favor is what magic consisted of in Ancient Kemet. In fact, in Kemet, there was a god of magic, and his name was Heka. He was usually depicted wearing a headdress with two hands held up. He was so embedded and present in all aspects of life that he almost seemed invisible due to his omnipresence. Therefore, you, too, are recommended to be aware of the omnipresence of magical forces and the ability to experience extraordinary outcomes as a result.

Health is a state of mind, body, and soul. These three aspects of the self must be healthy and in balance, if you want to ensure your continued health. According to Kemetism expert Muata Ashby, "Illness and dis-ease must be addressed at the soul level through the discipline of meditation, the mental level through studying and understanding the purpose of life... and at the physical level with the proper diet and exercise." Living a Kemetic lifestyle that includes Kemetic yoga, meditating on the laws of Ma'at, a Kemetic diet, and a spiritual study thus benefits your overall health and wellness. When you live in a healthy body, with a healthy mind and soul, you are living in harmony with yourself and in accordance with the laws of Ma'at. Therefore, a Kemetic lifestyle that seeks to improve your spiritual life is beneficial for all aspects of your existence.

HET HERU

THE TREE OF LIFE AND HOW
TO USE IT TO ACHIEVE
HIGHER CONSCIOUSNESS

The Tree of Life has been popularized by various religions. Evidence of its existence can be found in beliefs, religious texts, and geographical locations ranging from the Kabbalah, Buddhism, Celtic religion, Christianity, Turkish religion, the Assyrians, the Mayans, the Native Americans, Hinduism, Islam, and China. What these all have in common is their view of the tree of life as a connector between heaven and earth. Some cultures also see the tree of life as a force that binds families, cultures, and societies together.

Depictions of the tree of life in these cultures show a tree with its roots and its branches stretching low and high to eventually become a part of the circle within which it is enclosed. These visualizations embody how the tree of life is a tool to grow from our earthly roots to a level where we embrace the divine in the heavens. By using the tree of life in our spiritual journey, we can reach higher levels of spiritual awareness while creating a positive impact on those around us as we go about the motions of our daily lives. Using the tree of life as a tool for spiritual enlightenment allows us to embrace both heaven and earth.

The Kemetic tree of life also reaches from the earth toward the heavens. However, instead of a tree, it uses the form of an obelisk as its visual representation. The long column represents the various stages and multiple points of connection for the various gods and goddesses depicted in the creation story. The triangular-shaped Benben stone at the top of the structure represents the connection point to god the creator in the form of the rising sun, also known as Amen Ra or Amun Ra. It is upon the Benben stone that Ra alighted when he emerged from the waters of Nun. From this vantage point, he used the energy of vibration to create the world. As we go down from the Benben stone and travel along the column of the obelisk, we encounter different planes of existence, each associated with different principles. Each of these principles, or gods, in these planes of existence, represents a point along the human journey in their upward growth toward enlightenment. From the opposite direction, these points represent the creation journey downward from the ethereal toward increasing density. Aside from the obelisk with the pyramid-shaped Benben stone on top, the pyramid structure can also be seen as the tree of life. For this to happen, we must include the principles that form the base structure that enables creation to exist. These are the principles known as Nebethetepet and

Iusaaset. They come together to form time and space, creating a platform on which creation can exist. Together with Ra, they form a triangular structure that anchors the obelisk that represents the creation story.

When you use the obelisk or the pyramid as a structure to help you identify with the principles of creation and manifest them in your life, you must understand the order in which the principles appeared during the creation process. You will also need to embody the traits of these principles to face the challenges that each principle encountered during their coming into being. The challenges the principles faced throughout their lives and the ways in which they continuously met and overcame these is also a guideline to help you achieve greatness in your life by emulating the behaviors which helped them overcome challenges.

During the creation process, each principle emanated from the divine in a downward creation process. In your spiritual journey, you will engage each principle in the opposite order to the one they were created in. Each step that you take in ascending this ladder will bring you closer to your divinity. The more that you embody the positive aspects of the associated god or goddess, the greater your spiritual growth will be. The ultimate intention is for you to reach alignment with the creator god, Ra.

To aid you in your journey, let us take a deeper look at the process of creation and the principles in their order of appearance through the four planes of existence.

PLANES OF EXISTENCE

The Kemetic tree of life dates as far back as 4000 BCE and is represented by an obelisk or a pyramid to depict the path to spiritual enlightenment. The obelisk is divided into four planes of existence through which ascension must occur to reach a godly state. Each plane of existence represents a different human faculty that needs to be engaged and overcome in the journey to enlightenment.

Enlightenment is attained by overcoming the challenges encountered when facing the principles residing within each of the four planes of existence. Each principle is represented by a deity that represents the supreme force that it is in charge of.

By conquering each force within yourself as a spiritual seeker or initiate, you can move from mastery of the densest elements through to the more ethereal ones. Once you have mastered all 11 of these forces, you will reach a level of transcendence.

The forces are often felt as an inner drive or a desire. This will guide you toward understanding where you are on the journey, what you need to focus on, and how to master current challenges at any given moment. The principles are presented below in the order of creation, which is from the top down. Remember, though, that your spiritual journey will be an ascent from the bottom to the top. With each challenge that you overcome, you will face another that is higher on the tree of life. If you continue your spiritual journey, you will ascend until you attain the divinity of Ra.

NUN

The creation story starts in the first plane of existence, which is Nun, the undifferentiated consciousness. It is from out of these chaotic waters of Nun that Ra rises to sit on the Ben-ben stone. Nun is the absolute realm of the transcendental worlds.

RA, OR RE

Represented by a hawk-headed man with a sun disk on his head, Ra is the creator god. He created the god Shu and the goddess Tefnut after his emergence from the waters of Nun. Shu and Tefnut are air and moisture.

Ra represents the growth of living things through the power of the sun, which Ra embodies. Ra expresses himself in different forms, such as the rising sun—Amun Ra, and the setting sun—Tem Ra. In both of these states, Ra is getting ready to expend a great amount of energy for half of the day. As Amun Ra, he is preparing to light up the earth, bringing warmth and the capacity for growth and the creation of food via the effects of photosynthesis. As Tem Ra, however, he is about to get swallowed by the goddess of the sky, Nut. When Nut swallows Ra, she is in the form of the night sky. Here he will enter the underworld and spend the entire night traversing 12 gates and fighting the snake god Apep. He eventually emerges victorious in the form of the morning sun the following day.

While the obelisk represents the tree of life, Ra sits on

top of the Benben stone, which is found at the summit of the obelisk. This indicates his role as governor over all other deities found on the tree of life and on the creation journey. If you were to extend that Benben to the ground, you would find that it creates the shape of a pyramid at the ground level. That pyramid is anchored on either side by Nebe-thetepet and Iusaaset. They are the god and goddess who were there at the beginning of creation when Ra created the world. However, due to their role as anchors to the greater pyramid, they do not sit in the Nun plane. They are located in the lowermost plane of existence, the Ta.

DUAT

When Ra emerged from the waters of Nun, he emerged into the realm of the dead—the Duat. This is also referred to as the astral realm. Here, he emerged in the form that he takes when he enters this realm, which is Atum Ra or Tem Ra. When he was in this space, he went about bringing order to the world by creating the goddess Ma'at. It was here in the realm of the dead that he also created Ma'at's companion, Djehuti. In this realm, they are accompanied by Het-Heru, also known as Hathor—the goddess of the sky.

Duat, the causal plane, is the center of mental faculties such as consciousness and individuality. The principles of balance and order, as well as intellect, are found on this plane. Ma'at is balance and order, while Djehuti is the intellect. They are held together by the subtle force of order that is represented by Het-Heru.

MA'AT

Ma'at represents order. She is the goddess of truth, balance, and order. If you operate within the laws of Ma'at during the course of your lifetime, you will ensure that your life is in harmony with universal laws. These universal laws of Ma'at were put in place as the base structure needed by all existence. Ra brought Ma'at into being before the rest of creation was put in place. The Hermetic laws follow the principle of Ma'at, and being in alignment with them puts you in alignment with all of creation. This is why adopting these laws results in the ability to manifest your intentions faster than if you were in a state of disorder and chaos.

DJEHUTI OR THOTH

Djehuti, also known as Thoth, represents intellect. He is the god of wisdom, magic, the written word, and the moon. Thoth was the god of equilibrium and, therefore, worked closely with Ma'at. He was often represented as a man with the head of an Ibis or as a sitting baboon. His proximity to Ra is seen in the solar disk that he often wears on his head. He is a scribe and an advisor to the gods. He also rules over matters of justice on earth. He drives away Apophis or Apep, the snake of chaos that seeks to devour Ra every night. Thoth knows the past and the future, inclusive of the fate of each person from the moment of their birth. He numbers the days and years of humanity. After people die, he helps them pass through the hall of justice by providing them with magic spells to use against demons of the underworld.

Thoth is also known as Hermes Trismegistus. In that representation, he brought us the Hermetic Principles. These principles guide us on the ways that the laws of the universe operate. They show us how to behave if we want to engage with these laws for the purpose of bringing about change in our lives. He also brought us *The Emerald Tablets of Thoth*, which recount the last days of Atlantis and how his love of knowledge resulted in his transmutation from a man in Atlantis to a god in Egypt.

HET-HERU OR HATHOR

Hathor is the warrior goddess with the solar disk and bull's horns. As a warrior, she is part of the consort known as the *Eye of Ra*. This is the team that Ra sent to earth to restore order. One story about Hathor is that at one time, Sekhmet was sent to earth to punish humanity for wrongdoing. When Sekhmet arrived, she started killing people indiscriminately because they had all sinned. Ra tricked Sekhmet into drinking beer that looked like the blood of humanity. The alcohol caused her to fall asleep, and when she woke up, she was no longer Sekhmet but had taken on the form of the fun-loving Hathor.

Hathor is a fun-loving goddess whose gift to the world is gratitude. Observing religious rituals, praying, and partaking in festivals is her recipe for a good life. This attitude of gratitude that she teaches enables you to maintain the laws of Ma'at if you can cultivate it. The effects of gratitude continue into the afterlife, as it keeps your heart as light as a feather and, therefore, able to pass through the halls of judgment.

PET

Once the structures governing the universe had been put in place, Ra created Shu and Tefnut—air and moisture— either by spitting or sneezing them into existence. These were his children, whom he placed in the heavenly plane. They, in turn, created Geb and Nut—the earth and the sky.

Above the physical plane is Pet, the astral plane. It is on this level that dreams, ideas, thoughts, emotions, and imagination reside. The principles that you need to overcome to conquer this plane consist of air or ether, earth, water, and the heavens. You will therefore need to engage Shu, Geb, Tefnut, and Nut to enable you to do this.

SHU

Shu represents air, space, and ether. Shu is the god of light and a force for preservation. Preservation takes place in his presence. To understand this concept, consider how food that has been dehydrated can be preserved for consumption over a longer period of time.

His images depict him wearing ostrich feathers on his head. With one hand, he carries an ankh, which represents the breath of life. With the other hand, he carries a scepter, which represents power. He is often seen holding up the sky—Nut—with both hands while his feet rest next to Geb —the earth, who lies in repose on the ground. In some instances, Shu is depicted as a lion. Shu and Tefnut were also worshiped as a pair of lions.

TEFNUT OR TEFENET

Tefnut represents water and life force. She is the goddess of water, who brings about change through the introduction of moisture. In bringing about change, she creates the concept of time, which is used to differentiate the states before and after the change occurred.

She is seen with a uraeus serpent and a solar disk on her head. She has also been depicted with a crown of sprouting plants on her head. Like Shu, she carries an ankh and a scepter, representing life and power.

NUT

Nut represents heaven. She is the goddess of the sky. Nut and Geb were twins who were born holding each other close. When Ra ordered Shu to separate them, he held Nut above his head and left Geb lying at his feet. Nut's body keeps chaos at bay; otherwise, it would break through the skies and overcome the earth. This is the same chaos that threatens to consume Ra daily in the form of the snake Apep as he traverses the Duat. Because Ra had decreed that Nut could not give birth on any day of the year, a creative solution needed to be found for the pregnant Nut to give birth. Thoth devised a way to allow the heavily pregnant Nut to give birth while not defying Ra. He created five extra days using slivers of moonlight. Nut was able to give birth in succession during these extra days. The Kemetic calendar has 360 days and 5 extra days to cater for the full revolution around the sun. One can't help but wonder if those five extra days are the ones that Djehuti created to provide Nut extra days for giving birth. After all, the extra days do not fall easily into the well-divided Kemetic calendar.

Nut swallows Ra in the west at sunset and gives birth to him in the east at dawn. While traversing her inner body, Ra battles the demons of the underworld, including the snake Apep, whom Thoth helps to chase away. Nut provides fresh air to those souls that are in the underworld.

Nut is usually depicted as arched over the earth with her feet touching the ground on the left and her hands touching down to the right of the picture. She is also shown as a ladder between the earth and the heavens, which souls can climb up to get to the afterlife. Her body is often painted blue and covered with stars that represent the night sky.

GEB

Geb represents earth, as he is the god of the earth. He is the twin brother of Nut, the sky goddess.

His images depict him as a goose or as a man with a goose's head. Other images show him as a man wearing the Atef crown—a combination of the cone-shaped white Hedjet crown featuring curled ostrich feathers on either side.

TA

Geb and Nut had children who lived on the earthly plane following their difficult birth. They had to live on earth as Ra decreed that they were considered unfit to live on the heavenly plane due to the circumstances around their birth. These children of Nut became the protagonists in the stories that describe the main battles that humanity faces while living in the earthly realm. These are battles related to deception, envy, and the overcoming of evil through perseverance.

Ta is the physical plane of existence on which we experience life. This is the densest plane of existence. On this plane, you will find the forces known as Asar, Aset, Set, Nebthet, Heru Ur, Nebethetepet, and Iusaaset.

ASAR, AUSAR, OR OSIRIS

Asar represents the eternal soul. He is the god of fertility, life, death, and the underworld. His sovereignty over fertility includes the annual flooding of the river Nile and agricultural success. The latter is an association that cements his identity as being that of a green man. He was also depicted as a black man in a coffin. This is due to the fact that he was killed by his brother Set more than once, and each time his wife Aset worked hard to restore his life. The first time his brother killed him, he had been tricked into getting into a coffin. His brother then closed the lid and threw the coffin into the Nile River. However, rather than dying, Asar was eventually trapped into a pillar made of djed wood. Aset's rescuing him from the wooden pillar resulted in a second murder attempt by his brother. His pictures show him wearing the Atef crown with its recognizable ostrich-feather side detail while his hands are holding a crook and flail.

Asar is the husband-brother of Aset and the father of Anpu, or Anubis. Anpu is the son of Nephthys and was conceived when she was in disguise—this is how the story is told to cover up the fact that Asar had a child out of wedlock. Therefore, Nephthys, the goddess of the air, would have been in disguise as Auset, her sister and the wife of Asar. Asar is also the father of the twins Heru (younger Horus) and Bastet. Being the king of the underworld, all Pharaohs aspired to become like Asar upon their death.

ASET, AUSET, OR ISIS

Aset represents wisdom and intuition. She holds the title of "mother of all gods" as every Pharaoh was her child—Heru. Yet, upon death, these same pharaohs all aspired to become her husband—Asar. With her power to resurrect, she was able to bring her husband Asar back to life the first time that his brother Set killed him. After she did this, Set cut him into 14 pieces to ensure that he was truly dead. However, Aset gathered all his pieces together so that she could afford him a decent funeral. She even created a replacement body part after she could not find his penis, as it had been swallowed by a crocodile. It would be correct to say that it was due to her tireless actions that Asar was able to take his place as ruler of the underworld after his burial.

With her power to resurrect the dead, Aset was considered to be highly skilled in the magical arts. In this way, she earned the reputation of being able to heal all illnesses. You can call upon Aset to come to your aid in the most challenging circumstances, as the ancient Egyptians did. She overcame many difficult situations, and she helps those in need. Her ability to overcome was gained from Ra after she tricked him into revealing his real name to her. In so doing, she was able to bribe him into giving her his powers.

It has been said that images of Aset suckling Horus inspired early paintings of Mary and Jesus. Horus was conceived by Aset after she had created a phallus for him to ensure his body was complete at burial. Other images of her show her with a sun disk on her head that is carried by a throne or vulture headdress. She has also been depicted with a Shuty crown that carries the uraeus and the sun disk between two cow horns. However, the wearing of the Shuty may have to do with her conversion by the populace into the form of Hathor during the latter years of the Egyptian dynasties. Some of her images also show her wearing a three-stepped crown. She is associated with the moon, the Nile River, and the stars.

SET, SETH, OR SATET

He was the god of chaos, confusion, destruction, storms, foreign lands, eclipses, earthquakes, and violence. Set was the brother of Asar, to whom he brought a great deal of violent chaos during the course of his life. Set killed Asar during a power struggle for leadership over Egypt. As ruler over foreign lands, he was also a protector of hunters, soldiers, and trade caravans. He sowed confusion among enemy troops, resulting in success for Egypt's army. In later years, he was seen as a friend of Ra.

He is depicted as a long-snouted dog with long ears and a forked tail.

NEBTHET, OR NEPHTHYS

Goddess of the air, Nebthet, was married to Set and was the mother of Anubis. Anubis is the child of Asar, whom

Nebthet conceived after disguising herself as her sister Aset and seducing Asar.

Alongside Aset, she helped to resurrect Asar after Set had killed him. This earned her the title of "protector of the dead." She uniquely keeps watch over the organs in the canopic jars that are placed in the tomb alongside the dead when they are buried.

She is sometimes depicted with a basket on her head. She has also been depicted as a woman in mourning and as a hawk.

HERU-UR (HORUS THE ELDER)

Heru-Ur fought with Set after Set killed Asar for the throne. During the struggle, Heru-Ur lost his left eye. The eye was restored by Djehuti. Consequently, the moon goes through different phases, symbolizing the times when Heru-Ur's eye was complete up to the time he had no eye. As the lunar cycle resumes, his eye is restored to fullness. Therefore, the eye of Heru-Ur symbolizes restoration, health, and protection. The fully restored eye of Heru-Ur is symbolized by the *wedjat*, also known as the eye of Horus. Amulets of the eye of Horus are thought to be powerful.

In later years, though, Aset came to symbolize Hathor. During that season, Heru-Ur is depicted as a child or a husband of Hathor. The Greeks adopted Heru-Ur as Horus and, in later years, gave him the name Apollo. Therefore, any mention of Apollo from Greek texts can be seen as pertaining to Heru-Ur as a god.

Heru-Ur was represented by a falcon or by a winged sun disk. The winged Heru-Ur hovering over the head in an image indicated a king. In the form of a falcon, his right eye was the morning star of power. His left eye was the moon or the evening star, which had the strength to heal.

NBTH HOTEP, NEBETHETEPET, OR NEHMETAWY

Nebethetepet represents rest. Alongside motion, which is represented by Iusaaset, they create time and space. Thus, these two come together with Ra to form a triangle that is the foundation of time and space. This foundation enables Ra to create the world.

As Nehmetawy, she was the wife of Thoth and, at times, the wife of the snake god Nehebu-kau. Nehmetawy was the protector of the law and represented wisdom and justice. The name Nehmetawy means "the one who embraces those in need."

She is depicted as a woman in a long dress, sometimes carrying a child. On her head, she carries a crown made of the sistrum flanked by two uraei (uraei is the plural for uraeus. A *uraeus* is the Egyptian cobra; it was often placed as a symbol on the crowns of Egyptian royalty). A *sistrum* is a musical instrument shaped like an upside-down U with a handle on one end and bars placed horizontally across the U. The sound it makes is similar to shaking a tambourine.

Each uraeus on Nehmetawy's crown featured a sun disk on its head. This sistrum instrument that is her crown is similar to the one that Hathor is often seen carrying in her hand. Therefore, it has been assumed that there are more connections to be found between Nehmetawy and Hathor.

IUSAASET, IUSAS, OR SAOSIS

Iusaaset represents motion. She is also the goddess of the tree of life. The tree of life is the acacia tree because not only is it durable, but it is also edible and has medicinal properties. All deities, aside from Atum Ra, were born under the acacia tree, and Iusaaset is the grandmother to them all. Being the goddess of the medicinal acacia tree, she has the ability to remove every impurity from the body and to heal all diseases. Her ability to do so is stated in *The Book of Coming Forth By Day*, also known as *The Egyptian Book of The Dead*.

Alongside Atum Ra, she created the world as she is the goddess of creation. She is the utterer of the words that created the world.

She is also known as one of the 10,000 faces of Isis. In her images, she is depicted wearing a solar disk between two horns that sits on top of a vulture crown. In her hands, she carries an ankh and a scepter.

These are the gods and goddesses of creation. They are presented in the same order that they manifested. However, when you engage with them, you must do it from the bottom up as a tool to help you improve your life.

By meditating on the challenges they faced, you can

learn from them to help you engage your own struggles. You are also able to call upon them for guidance in the areas they have overcome. In this way, they become your guides through your life journey.

HEKA

❧ 3 ❧
HERMETIC SCIENCE MADE
EASY FOR EFFORTLESS
VITALITY AND ABUNDANCE

As mentioned previously, Hermetic Science was introduced to ancient Kemet and then ancient Greece by Hermes Trismegistus. The principles that he introduced are based on science. However, until recent scientific discoveries were made, these principles seemed to be steeped in belief with no scientific basis for their existence. Advances in modern science have brought scientific understanding to the level that spirituality and religion have always existed. This is the level whereby faith-based actions result in tangible outcomes. With this knowledge comes the understanding that the answering of prayers needs no longer be attributed to coincidence. Instead, prayer is a confirmation of the successful implementation of scientifically based actions. These actions need to be taken in alignment with Hermetic Science and the Seven Spiritual Principles.

Aside from being handed down in families and secret

societies, the Hermetic laws have been mostly lost to society over the millennia. In the past century, there have been occasions where these laws have surfaced in various forms to provide direction to those who were in a position to receive this knowledge. This book is one such avenue in that it brings attention to the Hermetic Laws in a direct manner. Other books that have done this include *The Secret* by Rhonda Byrne, *As A Man Thinketh* by James Allen, and *Think and Grow Rich* by Napoleon Hill, to name a few.

These books have tried to draw our attention to the fact that what we focus our attention on leads to growth in that area. This is true whether it is a positive or negative thought that we are focusing on. Our focus, combined with our emotions, serves as spiritual fertilizer for that thing to grow. The reason why this occurs is because of the Hermetic principles that the universe is aligned to. Our emotions serve as a source of energy that fuels our focus and thus activates the power of creation that exists within us. When we know and understand these universal laws, we are able to make changes in our lives that would have been difficult to bring about from a position of ignorance.

THE PRINCIPLE OF MENTALISM

This principle states that the universe is mental. It refers to the fact that there is a supreme consciousness that is in control of the entire universe. It is this supreme consciousness that controls the movement of the planets, the tides of the sea, and the rhythms of your body (Atkinson, 1908).

A belief in a higher spiritual power that created the universe is the foundation of most world religions. These religions attribute this higher spiritual power to the ability to control the world and ensure that all operations run smoothly, both on heaven and earth. Abrahamic religions have traditionally conceived of this figure as having human-like qualities. The euro-centric version of this has seen the depiction of God as an old bearded man floating on a cloud in the sky. Recent scientific events have helped us to shift our focus from a single physical entity that controls the world toward an understanding of the interconnectedness between living beings. Our previous personalization of the universal consciousness has proved to be a helpful method for directing the focus of our intentions by using the method of prayer. Its usefulness has risen from the idea that most people are unable to focus on the consciousness within them or from the universe. They are more easily able to direct prayers toward Allah, God, or Jesus and achieve similar outcomes.

The ancient Egyptians also used personalization of universal consciousness to assist them in directing their prayers toward their outcomes. They went further than a single god to focus on the various aspects that God embodies. By personalizing each aspect, they found a way to separate their needs into individual gods and goddesses that reflected what they would like to experience or see achieved in their lives. In this way, they were able to direct their prayer to that specific god or goddess who embodied the particular principles that they sought. This enabled them to hone in on the specific areas in which they needed improvement.

You can also use this approach to help with your prayer life and manifestation process. When you recognize the gods and goddesses that are in charge of the area of your life that you would like to bring growth to, you can focus on those principles that those deities embody. When you combine this with knowledge of the Hermetic principles, your capacity to achieve your desired outcome is enhanced due to your ability to make a more precise request. This is equivalent to having a focused prayer. Instead of praying to God for general goodwill in your life, you can pray to the god who helps you overcome the ego. In this way, you can use the principle of mentality to guide your ability to focus. In doing so, you will engage with universal consciousness and thus bring about the changes you seek.

Science has continued to provide us with evidence for the interconnectedness between all reality. The rediscovery of the atom and its component parts has revealed these to be the minute particles that make up all components of reality. This knowledge has changed the way that we look at all physical matter. The fact that the atom can be split to create a powerful explosion has created an awareness of the immense power that resides within the cells of every person.

Quantum physics has broken down these atoms further into electrons, quarks, and neutrons, whose states can be affected through mere observation. To have an effect on the state of the object, the observer needs to have an intention or an expectation for the object. What quantum theory tells us is that before an object exists in the real world, it lives in a state of potential. It may express its potential as either a wave or a particle, and once that potential has been expressed, it cannot revert. The moment of existence is preceded by an intention coinciding with an observation. The observer's intention, therefore, determines whether a particle will remain a particle or become a wave. From this, we learn that what you have in your mind in the form of intentions can impact the outcome of an observed event. This is the beginning of seeing the principle of mentalism in action.

These minute particles can also influence one another when they are not in close proximity to each other. As this concept has been explored further by the non-scientific community, it has moved the application of the resultant knowledge from the scientific realm to the spiritual. As a result, we have seen practitioners such as Dr. Joe Dispenza use quantum theory as a tool to guide the manipulation of an individual's existence by working with the information field (Dispenza, 2021). By recognizing the power of observation and intention, Dispenza encourages us to maintain positive thoughts and emotions if we want to have positive outcomes in our lives. His belief that you can influence your environment by harnessing the power of the mind is one that has been increasingly echoed by various spiritual and thought leaders.

At the base of these new teachings is the belief in the existence of a universal consciousness. Such consciousness is believed to connect all living matter, including each human being. Therefore, each person needs to understand that they can tap into the power of this universal consciousness by embracing a positive mindset and, thus, raising their vibration to resemble a frequency closer to a wave (the information field) than a particle (matter).

Embracing a positive mindset will ensure that you manifest positive results in your life. On the other hand, a focus on negative experiences will result in more negative life scenarios. The reason for this is that the universal consciousness responds to our emotions as a guide as to what we would like to experience. It then provides us with more experiences that are in alignment with the energy and emotion with which we made our request. Therefore, the emotions that you most strongly experience will guide your life in the direction of the thoughts that influence those emotions. This is one of the reasons why it is necessary to maintain inner peace within yourself by observing the Kemetic Principle of Ma'at. When you are living in Ma'at and make your requests from that level of peacefulness, you will welcome more experiences that engender this feeling within your life.

Therefore, we conclude that our engagement with the world around us can be influenced by our intention coupled with our emotions. This is how the principle has persisted, confirming to us thousands of years later that "the universe is mind."

THE PRINCIPLE OF CORRESPONDENCE

The principle of correspondence is embodied in the line "as above, so below" and can be further expanded to "as within, so without" (Atkinson, 1908).

The above refers to those things that govern the universe, while the below refers to individual experiences. These are reflections of each other. This stems from the belief that the universe is a hologram. If you have ever seen a hologram, you will have determined that each component of a hologram is a replica of the overall hologram. In the previous section, we discussed how atoms are the building blocks for all structural matter that forms the universe. However, if we look at how individual atoms behave, we find out that by splitting a single atom, we create a power that has the potential to destroy a city or provide an electricity supply to that same city. This stems from the continuous expansion process that takes place once the atom is split. The continuous expansion of the individual cell is similar to what is currently happening to our universe, which is continuously expanding. Therefore, the minuscule atom, which is a building block for the universe, has the same potential for continuous expansion as the universe itself.

When we take a step away from the behavior of that atom and we look at the universe graphically, we find an amazing hologram. The universe looks like the human brain cell. This is an amazing representation of the law of correspondence. The image of the universe brain that controls the cosmos is reflected in the human brain cell that controls our inner worlds.

This principle, however, goes beyond what the brain looks like and states that your individual circumstances reflect what is happening in the universe.

This belief is reflected in the practice of astrology, which bases its existence on this principle. Astrology proposes that the state of the universe at the time of your birth is a reflection of the life that you will have. Other practices that use this concept of the macrocosm being reflected in the microcosm are those that practice divination by means of asking a question at the same time as an action is performed. This takes place with the Chinese I Ching, which uses numbered coins in much the same way that traditional African spiritualists used bones, rocks, and other items to predict the future. They base their divinations on the belief that the moment that you ask a question and throw the coins, bones, rocks, etc., creates a divine coincidence between the question and the answer (Beitman, 2017). The answer is reflected in the items that are thrown, and by interpreting the layout of these items, you can decipher the answer to your question. This is because the spiritual realm from which your question emanates will have been reflected in the physical realm as represented by the thrown items.

Deepak Chopra goes so far as to state that all coincidences are meaningful and that we need to be aware of the synchronicity between events that occur together (Chopra, 2004).

This means that if you want to understand the world around you, you need to understand yourself as an individual because you are a reflection of your environment. Likewise, if you want to change your environment, work on changing yourself and then observe your environment to see how it reflects the changes that you have made. This comes about due to the synchronicity that exists between the two vastly different yet connected entities.

THE PRINCIPLE OF VIBRATION

Nothing rests; everything moves; everything vibrates (Atkinson, 1908).

Modern-day observations of science have concluded that it is not just gas particles that vibrate. Vibration is a phenomenon that is experienced by all physical items. The difference between items that look different despite having a similar chemical composition, such as solids, liquids, and gas, is due to the rate at which they vibrate.

When we look at the Kemetic creation story in light of this principle, we can understand the wisdom of why it starts off with the waters of Nun. These waters were an indication of pure potentiality that was able to move easily between states. Water is easy to observe as it moves between various states. It has a dense vibrational form called ice. When it moves to a higher vibrational manifestation, it becomes gas.

In this way, by observing the different states of water, we understand how the rate of vibration can influence the state of an object. Yet, one hundred years ago, scientists were not aware of the fact that everything vibrates. They assumed that solids were solid and nothing could permeate them. At that time, the principle of vibration was a reality to only a small group of knowledgeable individuals who have passed down this information to us throughout the ages.

Quantum physics has again allowed us to see that all items are made up of small vibrating atoms. We have come to understand that an armchair is a collection of densely packed atoms that vibrate at a slower rate than that of higher vibrational items.

This can apply to everything that you see. It is all energy that has been condensed to a physical form through the rate at which it vibrates. For items to interact directly with each other, they need to be vibrating at the same frequency. The frequency can render these items gas, liquids, or solids. Even solids can exchange atoms with representations from other states, as can be seen by the phenomenon of a white pair of shorts getting a green grass stain on them. Imagine a child playing outside wearing a clean pair of white shorts while kicking a ball around. The child falls on the grass, skidding forward slightly in the process. When they stand up, there is a green stain on their white shorts. Somehow there has been a transference of atoms from the grass to the shorts, resulting in the grass stain on the shorts. This is a simple example of the transfer of atoms between two solid items.

THE PRINCIPLE OF POLARITY

"Everything is dual; everything has poles; everything has its pair of opposites; like and unlike are the same; opposites are identical in nature, but different in degree; extremes meet; all truths are but half-truths; all paradoxes may be reconciled" (Atkinson, 1908).

This principle looks at everything as extremes of measurement between specific items. For example, love and hate are merely measurements of a single factor rather than two separate factors. This concept can be applied to everything. Through understanding the principle of polarity, one can move from one extreme to another by identifying what is being measured and moving along the method of measurement.

Here's an easy way to understand the application of this principle. Consider the actions that must be taken to warm up a room. The need for this comes about when you need to change its temperature from cold to hot. The cold is not what is being measured or changed. What is being adjusted is the temperature. Likewise, everything can be adjusted to its polar opposite. What you need to do is understand what it is that needs to be adjusted and how. Therefore, when you measure joy, you either have an abundance of it, or you have it in negative quantities, which we call sadness or depression. In order to live a life where joy is in abundance, you need to understand how to adjust your emotional barometer so that your joy reading goes up. This can be applied to everything that you experience in life. When you take this into account, it becomes another tool in the toolkit you use to change your life.

Taken from a different perspective, this also means that if you find yourself in a situation that does not suit you, be assured that the polar opposite of the situation exists. You need to find the method of measurement and then set about making the necessary changes that will bring about the polar opposite of the situation. One of the methods used to bring opposite states is the use of affirmations. The use of positive affirmations can shift your mindset and your environment over time from a negative to a positive implementation. The use of affirmations is done to supersede the evidence of your physical environment. By using sentences that describe the polar opposite of the situation you face, you acknowledge the fact that the situation you are speaking of exists. You acknowledge that every state has a polar opposite, and you call the other state into your existence through the principle of correspondence. You speak of the desired state as though it exists and, "as above" in your affirmative declaration, it will start to reflect "as below" in your experienced reality.

THE PRINCIPLE OF RHYTHM

Everything flows, out and in; everything has its tides; all things rise and fall; the pendulum swing manifests in everything; the measure of the swing to the right is the measure of the swing to the left; rhythm compensates (Atkinson, 1908).

This indicates that there is a tendency for things, such

as events and circumstances, to flow in a certain direction. However, after some time, they will change direction and flow back in the opposite direction. Therefore, if circumstances are not in alignment with your chosen direction, you may practice patience as you prepare for a shifting of circumstances. Circumstances will shift, but you will need to be prepared for when they do so that you can take advantage of them.

A simple example of this is a farmer who would like to plant some pumpkins. If he does this in the middle of winter, these seeds are unlikely to grow, let alone provide a harvest. However, there are things that he can do to prepare for summertime when the weather will be conducive to a bumper crop of pumpkins. He could find the right seed, he could prepare the ground, and he could make sure that his water supply is in place. He could also start planting seedlings indoors so that he has a head start on other farmers in the area, allowing him to harvest and sell his pumpkins earlier in the season before the market for pumpkins becomes saturated. This will lead to great success for the farmer.

The farmer's success will not come about by chance, though. It will have been a result of careful observation. This requires tracking the seasons and knowing the optimal conditions for growing pumpkins. Even in the middle of winter, when the growth conditions are at their worst, he will have held onto the belief that the seasons will change. He believes that the weather will change, and one day, it will be the middle of summer. His knowledge of the change of seasons and of farming cycles makes him aware that the middle of summer is a time during which it will be too late to plant his pumpkins. Therefore, the farmer prepares and waits out the winter season until the weather is optimal for his needs.

Surfers understand this concept as well. They are willing to swim out to sea and wait for the ultimate wave that they can then surf to shore. They do not surf every single wave, as some are too small to make an impact. However, by being in the right position and waiting, they are living in a state of belief that the right wave will come. When the right wave does come, the surfer will move to get into a position that will allow them to take advantage of the wave and thus ride it to shore.

What we learn from this is that we too should be like surfers or the pumpkin farmer. We need to position ourselves in a place where we can take advantage of the changes in circumstances when they do occur. This means that we must be prepared, we must be observant, and we must be able to take immediate action when the opportunity presents itself. Failing to do so might mean that, if we are surfers, we miss out on the big wave and end up having to ride a lesser wave to shore. If we are farmers, it could mean only harvesting pumpkins once in the season instead of twice.

Another way to look at this is that you can choose to follow the path of least resistance by being observant and leveraging the time and energy that is available to you.

THE PRINCIPLE OF CAUSALITY

Every cause has its effect; every effect has its cause; everything happens according to law; chance is but a name for
law not recognized; there are many planes of causation, but
nothing escapes the law (Atkinson, 1908).

Every action that we take has a consequence; therefore,
we need to take the right actions if we want to achieve the
outcomes that we want. By the same token, we need to be
aware of the potential for unintended consequences and try
to avoid engaging in any actions that may lead to them.

From a scientific perspective, this has been enshrined in
Newton's third law of physics, which states that every
action has an equal and opposite reaction. We can observe
this in physics when we see a tennis ball bouncing against a
wall. The wall does not give in and allow the ball to go
through it. Instead, the ball bounces back from the wall
with the same or similar speed and impact to that with
which it approached the wall. When we consider the fact
that all matter is made up of vibrating energy, we are then
invited to factor universal consciousness into this equation.

Factoring in consciousness means that the impact of
opposing forces can be applied not just to our actions but to
our thoughts and our emotions as well. Therefore, if you
hate football with a vengeance, to the extent that you reject
it vehemently, you are likely to encounter football more in
your life than if you had no emotion toward it at all. This is
because your emotions are like throwing a football at the
wall of the universe, and the universe will provide back to

you what you are throwing at it. Therefore, you will receive more football.

By the same token, if you smile at strangers on the street, you are more likely to have strangers smiling back at you. You are receiving the thing that you are giving out. Your action, which is the cause, is receiving its effect, which is the result of the action. What you receive back is equivalent to what you give.

This principle has been enshrined in various religions as the law of sowing and reaping, which states that you will reap what you sow, or the law of karma, which states that your actions will be returned to you. Some texts state that you will reap in multiples, the same way that a farmer who sows one seed of corn will reap several heads with a few hundred seeds on them. Therefore, these texts state that the impact of your actions is multiplied when returned to you.

This is a universal principle that we should not ignore if we want to have pleasant outcomes in life. We need to be conscious of the potential to sow bad seed. Therefore, if we do find ourselves engaging in practices that we do not want to impact us negatively in the future, we need to do our utmost to address these and to correct them so that we neutralize the potential impact of future negative karma.

Sometimes we are surprised to reap good seed in unexpected ways. At those times, we should be happy that at some point in the past, we sowed a good seed that is finally coming into fruition and is ready for harvest.

THE PRINCIPLE OF GENDER

Gender is in everything; everything has its masculine and feminine principles; gender manifests on all planes (Atkinson, 1908).

Creativity comes about as a result of the interaction between the masculine and feminine aspects. This involves the giving of a seed and the receiving of a seed in circumstances that enable it to be nurtured for a fruitful gestation period. The seed that you plant could be time, money, or your physical effort. That seed needs to be planted into fertile ground and watered for it to bear fruit.

Imagine you are an artist and have an idea (a seed) that you then put onto a canvas. By nurturing that canvas through the addition of various layers and colors from your paint palette, you will eventually see results. These results will be in the form of a beautiful painting that is appreciated by others.

Every person has both masculine and feminine traits within them, whether that individual is biologically male or female. It is the activity that is being undertaken by the individual that determines whether the traits being displayed are masculine or feminine. Traits such as creativity and receptiveness tend to be feminine traits, while logic and leadership are masculine traits. These traits operate best when they operate together. The traits support each other. Creativity needs guidance, and leadership requires something to lead.

The ability to display these traits is evident not just in

people but also in events and objects. For example, events that result in new directions display masculine energy, while events that nurture and grow societies are feminine in nature.

This needs to be recognized in all aspects and all planes of existence. Once you understand the gender of an event, organization, or object, it can guide how you interact with it. As gender is the basis for creativity and regeneration, it is beneficial to apply knowledge of genders during the process of creation. What this means is that, depending on the gender that you are faced with, you can either choose to direct or nurture the event. This will enable creation to occur.

Our mental faculties as human beings are also seen as having both masculine and feminine traits. This is seen in the existence of both a conscious and a subconscious mind. While the conscious mind absorbs new information, the subconscious mind uses existing information to engage in daily activities and make unconscious decisions. In order to create new output, both the conscious and subconscious minds need to be engaged. The role of the subconscious mind is to take care of daily activities such as breathing and the digestion of food. You do these things without thinking. The subconscious mind also enables huge changes to occur without you being aware of it on a conscious level. The way that the subconscious mind does this is by ensuring that you remain consistent in the decisions you make daily in accordance with your prevailing belief systems. According to *The Power of The Subconscious Mind* by Joseph Murphy, you can choose to impact your subconscious mind by actively feeding it new information and beliefs. If you do this persistently over a period of time, you will effectively be using the masculine traits of your brain to impact the feminine traits. This will result in creating a new paradigm and reality for yourself.

From a business perspective, if you are an artist, you will work better with masculine energies that can steer you in the directions that can lead to the growth of your artwork through increased sales while you focus on your creativity. In this instance, the creativity is a feminine energy, and it requires masculine energy in order to grow. If you are a business person with a great strategy and vision for the future, you may find that you are unable to move this strategy forward without including people with creative energies and outlooks in your business. These people will take your business strategy and use their creativity to bring it to life by growing the idea from a seed to its full potential.

Therefore, for success to occur, both masculine and feminine energies need to be optimized through a balanced contribution from both sides.

Through viewing the Hermetic principles, we have seen how the science practiced in ancient Kemet has not been lost to humanity. It has been preserved through the ages and reinforced through scientific discoveries that have taken place over the last century. As a result, humanity is coming to realize we can have a greater impact on our individual destinies than we initially believed was possible. All we need to do is tap into the universal consciousness with the help of the seven Hermetic laws.

To further help you in accessing this consciousness, it would be beneficial to take time daily to reflect on the Hermetic principles and what they each mean. Once you have memorized them all, start to think of ways that these principles can be applied in your life. Make note of your current circumstances in comparison to the circumstances that you would like to bring about. Identify the methods that you can use to bring about your intended consequences. Write these methods down and take simple actions daily to help you implement these methods. Over time, compare your life with the way it is right now and determine what changes have come about as a result of implementing the laws as a means of attaining your desires.

TEFNUT

✵ 4 ✵

KEMETIC ASTROLOGY AND A DEEPER UNDERSTANDING OF THE PERSONALITY TYPES INHABITING THIS WORLD

There are 12 star signs in Kemetic astrology. Unlike western astrology, these are not spread out consecutively over 12 parts of the year. Instead, they divide the year into 36 equal parts, referred to as *decans*, and these divide the 360 days of the Egyptian year. The year had 120 days in each of its three seasons. Every season contained four months of 30 days each. A bonus five-day month was added each year to account for the additional days in the earth's revolution around the sun. These days were used as celebration days, and they brought the actual days marked by the ancient Egyptians to 365. The calendar depicted in this circular manner was first seen on the ceiling of an Egyptian Temple of Hathor in what has now become known as "The Dendera Zodiac."

This Dendera calendar used astrology from the basis of the Hermetic Law of Correspondence: "As Above So Below." Thus, it exposed the Kemetic belief that occurrences on earth are reflected in the movements of the heavenly bodies. The modern-day application for this is in the form of astrological signs, which we have become accustomed to seeing in newspapers and magazines. In this way, the Kemetic practice has survived through the ages due to its adoption by the Greeks, who subsequently adapted it for a Eurocentric market. The familiarity of identifying one's birthday in accordance with a star sign has become a popular and accepted method to help define personality archetypes. This method of defining personalities uses methods that are similar to the ones that were used in ancient Egypt.

The ancient Egyptians also used astrological observations to correctly predict major events, such as the annual flooding of the Nile. This was an important event for them, as it preceded their agricultural season and defined the processes that were to be followed for the rest of the year. Therefore, knowing that the flood season was approaching gave them adequate time to prepare for planting. Having used the astrological method successfully in agriculture, it was, therefore, logical and scientific to use similar observations to predict events in the lives of individuals.

The Kemetic astrological calendar can still be used in the present day. By identifying the correlation between the gods and goddesses and their representations within the constellations at various times of the year, we can predict and interpret events. According to Cyril Fagan, who was a member of England's Royal Astronomical Organization in 1798, Kemetic astrology was the precursor for modern astrology (Afrikaiswoke, 2021). Modern-day astrology still follows the allocation of star signs to individuals at birth. This is done in accordance with the constellation that was prominent at the time of their birth. From a Kemetic perspective, it is the personality types of the gods and goddesses that are indicated at the birth times which are important. These reveal the personality types and expectations that we can have of the individual or the event that is birthed at that time.

In alphabetic order, the Kemetic star signs are Amun Ra, Anubis, Bastet, Geb, Horus, Isis, Mut, Osiris, Sekhmet, Seth, The Nile—or Satis, and Thoth.

FINDING YOUR SIGN

To identify which star sign was in effect at the time of your birth, use the table below. The first column indicates a range of days. From this column, you need to identify the days that your birthday falls into. On the same line, the table indicates your star signs in accordance with the range of days during which you were born. The third and final column indicates which signs are compatible with your sign. Therefore, reading along the row will provide you with an indication of both your sign as well as the star signs it is compatible with.

Date of Birth	Sign	Compatibility
January 1–7	The Nile or Satis	Amun-Ra, Set
January 8–21	Amun Ra	The Nile/Satis, Horus
January 22–31	Mut	Amun-Ra, Thoth
February 1–11	Amun Ra	The Nile/Satis, Horus
February 12–29	Geb	Set, Horus
March 1–10	Osiris	Isis, Thoth
March 11–31	Isis	Thoth, Osiris
April 1–19	Thoth	Bastet, Isis
April 20–May 7	Horus	Bastet, Geb
May 8–27	Anubis	Bastet, Isis
May 28–June 18	Seth	Geb, The Nile/Satis
June 19–28	The Nile or Satis	Amun-Ra, Set
June 29–July 13	Anubis	Bastet, Isis
July 14–28	Bastet	Sekhmet, Horus
July 29–August 11	Sekhmet	Bastet, Geb
August 12–August 19	Horus	Bastet, Geb
August 20–31	Geb	Set, Horus

Figure One

Date of Birth	Sign	Compatibility
September 1–7	The Nile or Satis	Amun-Ra, Set
September 8–22	Mut	Amun-Ra, Thoth
September 23–27	Bastet	Sekhmet, Horus
September 28–October 2	Seth	Geb, The Nile/Satis
October 3–17	Bastet	Sekhmet, Horus
October 18–29	Isis	Thoth, Osiris
October 30–November 7	Sekhmet	Bastet, Geb
November 8–17	Thoth	Bastet, Isis
November 18–26	The Nile or Satis	Amun-Ra, Set
November 27–December 18	Osiris	Isis, Thoth
December 19–31	Isis	Thoth, Osiris

Figure One (Continued)

ASTROLOGICAL PERSONALITY TYPES

The personality type associated with each sign is a reflection of the element, god, or goddess that the sign represents. Here we will examine each sign by identifying the heavenly bodies that influence these signs as well as the personality traits that each sign displays. Identifying the heavenly bodies is important due to the fact that individual personality traits become more pronounced when these heavenly bodies are located in that particular constellation in the sky. In the same way that western astrology can take note of the effects of planetary configurations, such as how Mars being in Aries can impact the lives of those born in the sign of Aries, so too can this awareness play out in Kemetic astrology.

To benefit from the knowledge that is available to you during these modern times, you must first understand how the modern star signs correspond to the Kemetic star signs. When you reference the astrology pages and websites, you can then look for information that tells you what star sign a certain planet or heavenly body is currently located in. By understanding which star sign you were born under, in conjunction with the planets that impact these star signs, you can respond to situations differently. You can plan your important events for those times when the planets that are supportive of your star sign are active in the night sky. You can also gain a greater insight into your personality and how to engage with others.

As you get into the habit of reading information that pertains to which constellation certain planets are located in at a given time, you will find that the currently named western star signs do not always correspond to all the times that their constellations are dominant in the sky. The manner in which Kemetic astrology repeats the star signs at different intervals throughout the year is a better indicator of activities taking place in the night skies than a simplified astrological grouping that vaguely covers a month at a time. The section below provides insight into how the western star signs correspond to the Kemetic star signs. Following this, there will be a section that examines the benevolent planets for each star sign and how these impact the personality types of people or events born under those star signs. Please note that the correspondences below are not related to your birthday and related sign but should be used as a way to interpret statements such as "Venus is in Sagittarius" in your own life. If Sagittarius is Hapi, then if you were born under the Kemetic sign of Hapi, this will impact you. However, being a Sagittarius star sign does not translate into being born under the sign of Hapi. It is advisable to rather use the table from the previous section if you want to know what Kemetic star sign you fall under. The date ranges for each sign are for a few weeks at different times of the year; therefore, you need to map your date of birth to your specific star sign if you want to gain maximum benefit from the information provided.

CORRESPONDENCE BETWEEN CONSTELLATION NAMES

- If Aquarius is the dominant constellation, then the effective Kemetic star sign is Sekhmet.
- If Aries is the dominant constellation, then the effective Kemetic star sign is Osiris or Ausar.
- If Cancer is the dominant constellation, then the effective Kemetic star sign is Bastet.
- If Capricorn is the dominant constellation, then the effective Kemetic star sign is Horus.
- If Gemini is the dominant constellation, then the effective Kemetic star sign is Seth or Set.

- If Leo is the dominant constellation, then the effective Kemetic star sign is Anubis.
- If Libra is the dominant constellation, then the effective Kemetic star sign is Geb.
- If Pisces is the dominant constellation, then the effective Kemetic star sign is Isis or Auset.
- If Sagittarius is the dominant constellation, then the effective Kemetic star sign is Hapi.
- If Scorpio is the dominant constellation, then the effective Kemetic star sign is Mut.
- If Taurus is the dominant constellation, then the effective Kemetic star sign is Amun Ra.
- If Virgo is the dominant constellation, then the effective Kemetic star sign is Thoth or Djehuty.

BENEVOLENT PLANETS AND THEIR PERSONALITY TYPES

These are the personality types of each star sign:

- Amun Ra is influenced by the sun and Saturn. Those born under this sign are great leaders who make wise decisions. They have an optimistic approach to life and are confident and polite in nature.
- Anubis is influenced by Mercury. With Anubis being the guardian of the underworld, it is no surprise that people born under this sign have introverted personalities. They have a creative

side to their personalities, which they tend to express in a confident and exploratory manner.

- Bastet is influenced by the sun and the moon. Charming and affectionate, Bastet people tend to avoid conflict due to their sensitive personalities. They rely on their intuition to guide them with this. They are deeply loyal and devoted to their partners.

- Geb is god of the earth; therefore, those born under this sign are influenced by earth. People born under this sign are faithful and reliable friends. They can be perceived as over-emotional and sensitive; however, their open nature makes them attractive to others. They can seem shy to those who are not close to them.

- Horus is influenced by the moon and the sun. People born under this sign are inspirational leaders who are both hardworking and motivational. Their courage and optimism are contagious, making their ambitious examples easy to follow.

- Isis (Aset) is the goddess of nature. Her sign is influenced by the Moon, Earth, and Uranus. These people work well within a team due to their straightforward yet sociable nature. They are honest with a sense of humor and a romantic flair.

- Mut is influenced by the sun. People born under this sign make great parents due to their protective and affectionate nature. They make good leaders as they are goal-oriented and focused while being generous and loyal.

- Osiris (Asar) is influenced by Pluto and the sun. Those born under this sign are very determined. This can sometimes be perceived as aggressive and selfish. However, their persistent and independent approach to life makes them good leaders who are often valued for their intelligence and vulnerability.

- Sekhmet is influenced by the sun. People born under this sign are considered to have dual personalities due to their nature vacillating between free-spiritedness and extreme discipline. These people have a deep sense of justice and, if called upon to instill it, will do so with precision.

- Seth (Set) is influenced by Mars. Set people are perfectionists who enjoy being the center of attention. Their bold personalities push them toward challenging situations that allow them to shine further.

- The Nile (Satis) is influenced by the moon and Uranus. People born under this star sign are considered to be intuitive as a result of their great observational skills. This is a peace-loving sign that avoids arguments. Those born under the Nile sign display great wisdom based on their capacity for exercising logic.

- Thoth is influenced by the Moon and Mercury. Like the god that inspires the star sign, people born under it are wise and enjoy learning. Constantly seeking improvement, these people tend to be courageous, energetic, and inventive. Thoth is considered to be a very romantic sign. Knowing your star sign and the signs that it is compatible with will make it easier for you to make decisions about how to engage with different people. It will help you understand them better and know what personality traits to leverage in both business and personal partnerships.

You can use this information to help you decide on the best dates to perform certain activities. It is advisable to choose days that are compatible with your star signs as much as you can. If you are unable to select the date for an event, you can still make the most of your experience of the event. By examining the date and the associated star sign of the event, you can understand the personality type of the occurrence and how to best engage with it.

ASAR

5

THE KEMETIC DIET AND HOW
IT CAN SKYROCKET YOUR
SPIRITUAL CONNECTION

"You are what you eat." The truth of this adage can be found by looking at the people around us. We will see in them not just the physical evidence of the foods they eat, but the emotional and psychological impacts that these foods have as well.

Another popular adage, "Let your food be your medicine," is reflective of the lives that we should strive toward living. It is also indicative of the lives that most initiates lived in ancient Kemet as they went about their daily lives, aligning with the laws of Ma'at and taking their sustenance from the environment.

They were at an advantage over us today in that their environment made it easier for them to eat a healthy, balanced diet that both sustained and nurtured them. The food that they ate was not processed and was in its most natural form. This ensured that they received the maximum amount of divine energy from their food.

Energy comes to the earth from the sun—Ra. Plants absorb that solar energy through the process of photosynthesis and convert it into food. When animals eat plants, they absorb the sun's energy from the plants themselves. By eating animals, humans have been attempting to derive energy from a source that is three steps removed from the giver of energy to the earth. Digesting this food requires us to use more energy to access the limited supply provided by these animal sources. In the course of events, we have also developed diseases that are linked to the processing of these foods. The cause of such disease is that our bodies were not initially designed to process these foods. Some of the foods are toxic to us, while others remain in our digestive tracts for so long that they become rancid and start to rot inside our bodies while our intestines try to push the remains out. The lack of digestive fiber in the refined foods we consume makes it difficult for our bodies to accomplish this task. Over time, the residue in our digestive tracts builds up, resulting in illnesses. With the link between the brain and the large intestine that is formed by the vagus nerve, the illness in your gut has a direct impact on your emotions, mental health, and vitality. The microbes that are produced in your gut have a direct impact on your immune system through their impact on inflammation.

THE MODERN URBAN (or Standard Western) Diet and Its Pitfalls

Our modern diet has become increasingly removed

from nature. When it comes to drinking, many of us tend to consume great amounts of alcoholic beverages. We also consume drinks with a high caffeine content, in addition to carbonated beverages that have been sweetened with artificial or refined sweeteners. The intake of pure water is often non-existent. All this leads to a very acidic body and gastrointestinal composition, which is vulnerable to disease. Some of the effects of too much acid in the digestive system include headaches, depression, acne, brittle hair and nails, kidney stones, and reduced muscle mass. Of course, there are those of us that demonstrate incredible willpower and mindfulness over our dietary consumption. However, we must still remain aware and vigilant of any potentially harmful products we may encounter.

On a daily basis, many of us tend to consume fast food. These are often high in refined carbohydrates and meat content. The meat sources have often been force-fed with sources such as soya to fatten them up. To further aid this process, the animals are either fed or injected with growth hormones. This happens in overpopulated environments, leading to the spread of disease among livestock. As a result, they are given antibiotics that end up in the human body when the meat is consumed. The antibiotics in our bloodstream from these animals result in resistance to antibiotics over time. The result is that when some people get sick, they are not easily treatable with regular antibiotics, making them more susceptible to disease and requiring toxic levels of chemicals and antibodies to combat illness. The presence of antibiotics in the digestive tract additionally serves to kill off any beneficial microbes that live in the digestive tract for the purpose of aiding in the digestion process and balancing the gut flora. This leaves people vulnerable to excessive growth of harmful gut bacteria and the prevalence of fungal diseases caused by organisms like Candida.

Fast food is not often served with vegetables or salads. The lack of greenery combined with the refined nature of the carbohydrates in the food makes it difficult for the food to pass through the digestive system. The food is often low in nutritional content, requiring the body to work harder to absorb nutritional value from the food. Over time, such a diet leads to diseases that originate in the gastrointestinal tract and spread to other parts of the body via the vagus nerve.

The presence of undigested and fermenting food in the body results in individuals feeling sluggish and depressed, leading to an increase in mental health issues among those who consume such a diet.

FOOD IN ANCIENT KEMET

So what food was eaten in ancient Egypt? Was all the food they ate part of what we now call the Kemetic diet? If not, what was included in the Kemetic diet? And what foods have we been consuming that we should seek to minimize or eliminate from our diet for us to achieve optimal health and alignment with the divine within ourselves?

.   .   .

SPIRITUAL INITIATES

Ancient Egypt had citizens who played different roles in society. The priests and priestesses of the temples were continually striving to live in the purest form of alignment to Ma'at and divine purpose. They were on the spiritual path. Therefore, the diet that they consumed was purely vegan, with a raw food diet comprising a large part of their eating plan. They shied away from grains such as wheat and corn. For them, even pulses such as lentils and beans were considered starch; therefore, the initiates of the temple did not consume these. They instead sought to eat food that was as green as possible, allowing them to absorb the full intensity of the sun's energy that had been trapped through photosynthesis. In fact, their intention when choosing their food was to be as green as Asar. Asar was a green-colored god who was the embodiment of Ra. They believed that by eating green foods, they could practice theurgy by emulating Asar. This plan of eating enabled them to live in a state of high vibrational awareness, not weighed down by the impact of digesting animal products.

As somebody who is reading this book because you are on a spiritual path, you too may benefit from following the diet of the priests and priestesses of the temples. This will allow you to live in balance with nature. However, it is not advisable to immediately change from a modern urban diet to the Kemetic diet that was followed by the initiates. To prevent your body from experiencing withdrawal symptoms and distress, it is best to make gradual changes to your diet until you reach your goal. We will outline how to go about this once we have looked into the food that was eaten by the general populace of ancient Egypt. You must also always take responsibility for your own diet and well-being.

The General Populace

Regular citizens of Kemet followed mainly a pescatarian or a flexitarian diet. Red meat and poultry were included in their diet in small quantities, as was alcohol. The staple diet of Kemet was bread. This was a supplement to their mainly vegetarian diet of pulses, vegetables, and fruit. These were eaten uncooked, and the custom of eating vegetables uncooked remains to this day.

Meat was consumed, although not in the large daily quantities that our modern diet embraces. Beef would be prepared through stewing or by drying it out after salting it for preservation purposes. Sheep, goats, and, very rarely, pork were eaten less often than beef. From analyzing remains found in mummies, we find that wildlife in the form of gazelle, hyena, and mice also found their way into their diet.

Poultry, such as quail, geese, ducks, partridges, cranes, pigeons, doves, flamingoes, pelicans, and chickens, was prepared by roasting or preserving through the use of salt and dehydration.

Fish was the most regular non-vegetarian aspect of the diet. This was consumed after roasting it. Alternatively, it was eaten in its preserved form, which was salted and dried.

Animal products, such as eggs, milk, and cheese from

cows and goats, were consumed. Honey was used as a food sweetener instead of the artificial and refined sweeteners that we use today.

Alcohol was consumed in the form of beer and wine.

The vegetables they consumed had a high legume content, with lentils and other pulses forming a major part of their diet.

A look into king Tutankhamun's burial site reveals the wide array of vegetarian food that he took with him to the afterlife and, therefore, the food that he consumed during his lifetime. These foods included almonds, figs, pomegranates, dates, garlic, fenugreek, coriander seeds, chickpeas, watermelon, lentils, and emmer wheat.

DIETARY GUIDE FOR MODERN-DAY KEMETICS

The Kemetic diet proposed here is the one that was followed by the priests and priestesses of ancient Kemet. It is a raw vegetarian diet that consists mostly of fruit and vegetables and excludes the consumption of flesh, such as fish, poultry, or livestock.

WHY THE KEMETIC DIET?

Sages of ancient Kemet recognized that physical and spiritual health were intertwined. Following the Kemetic diet may contribute to a longer, healthier, and more enjoyable life. You could potentially avoid spending your sunset years going in and out of hospitals, attending to the cumulative effects that a bad diet could have on your health. Such ill effects include diabetes, high blood pressure, and cancer. Instead, the Kemetic diet enables you to consume food that allows you to live in Ma'at and promotes your spiritual journey.

Furthermore, the Kemetic diet reduces the amount of disease-causing acids in your body. Your body functions best when it maintains a slightly alkaline level of 7.4 on the pH scale (Adams, n.d.). The consumption of fruit and vegetables in large quantities can contribute toward stabilizing the pH of your body, keeping your blood oxygenated, and thus making you less susceptible to disease. An alkaline diet also includes the addition of nuts, seeds, legumes, and herbal teas.

BENEFITS

The Kemetic diet removes the source of most food allergies from the diet. It allows us to absorb our energy from food sources that have immediately harvested energy from Ra. It follows, therefore, that pursuing a Kemetic diet results in higher energy levels and a reduced incidence of disease. Consuming the purest form of nutrition allows you to live in alignment with the divine by being as green as Asar.

Adopting a plant-based Kemetic diet reduces the likelihood of developing diseases such as hypertension, high cholesterol, cancer, and obesity. Moreover, a plant-based diet boosts the immune system, providing protection against seasonal illnesses such as colds and flu. It increases the energy levels in the body and reduces the likelihood of depression, stress, and associated mental disorders.

WHAT TO EAT

Try to eat fresh fruit and vegetables as much as you are able. In addition to their nutritional value, these add fiber to the diet, which is conducive to a well-functioning digestive system. If possible, eat fruit and vegetables raw. However, do not eat them at the same time. Rather, eat fruit about 30 minutes before you eat vegetables. In instances whereby you are unable to eat vegetables raw and they need to be cooked, try not to overcook them. In the case of green vegetables, such as kale and spinach, grill them or use the steaming method to cook these. In this manner, their natural goodness will be maintained as much as possible. To create alignment between your body and the fruits and vegetables that you eat, only try to eat food that is in season. Eating food that is out of season necessitates that food is transported long distances from regions other than the one that you are in. These foods are not in alignment with your body rhythms as they were grown in a different area. As a result, they may cause your body internal stress.

In the same way that a 30-minute period should be observed between consuming fruit and vegetables, you should take care within your diet not to eat any more than three different types of food at a time. This is to reduce the strain on your digestive tract.

If you have the necessary facilities, you can sunbake your food. This is the healthiest form of cooking, as it further harnesses the sun's energy for absorption into your body.

Drink as much water as necessary for your body so that you avoid feeling thirsty. Adding a slice of lemon or lime to the water is advisable, as it will help you neutralize any acidity that could be present in your body. This is great for your overall health. If you choose to consume fruit juices, avoid those that are carbonated or that contain a high sugar content. Rather, consume coconut water, pure fruit juice, and herbal teas. After drinking your liquids, try to wait an hour before eating. It is best that eating and drinking do not take place at the same time.

Try and get used to the practice of juicing. You can make green juice using leafy greens and cucumbers. Add some orange- or red-colored fruit for additional flavor. Apples also make great additions to your juice. Try to consume the juice as close as possible to the time of squeezing it.

To snack on, consider eating nuts such as raw almonds, which are rich in nutrients. They are packed with calcium, magnesium, protein, and vitamin E. To consume almonds, soak them overnight in water. This will make it easier for your body to absorb the natural goodness from them. When eating nuts, try to avoid eating them at the same time as moist foods, such as fresh fruit. However, these may be eaten with dried fruits, as they have a similar lack of water content and will require the same effort to digest. You can also include seeds, such as pumpkin seeds and sunflower seeds, as additional snack items.

GRAINS, *Legumes, and Root Vegetables*

Starches are included in the Kemetic diet in the form of root vegetables, legumes, and grains. They are considered a staple part of the meal; however, they should not be consumed in large quantities. Instead, they need to be adequately balanced with green vegetables, especially those that contain direct energy from the sun.

The best diet for your body is one that consists purely of fruit and vegetables, with a high emphasis on raw food. However, trying to immediately implement a raw food diet after having consumed a modern diet for your entire life can be detrimental to your body. Your body will have become accustomed to the enzymes and minerals that it derives from these foods, and a sudden change could lead to withdrawal symptoms. If not managed properly, abruptly changing the diet toward veganism could result in being unable to maintain your resolve. Reverting to your previous habits can promote the tendency to consume more addictive substances than you consumed before, such as meat and sugar.

A LUCID DIET

A successful transition will result in your partaking in what is known as a lucid diet. This diet consists of sprouted seeds, nuts, fruit, vegetables, and legumes. A lucid diet promotes clarity of mind and increased willpower and provides you with an overall sense of harmony.

To be successful in your transition, try and reduce foods that are of less benefit to you. Cut out foods that are harmful by substituting healthy alternatives that will allow your body to wean off the substances that it has become accustomed to. With reduced intake, you will be able to move toward full veganism and a raw food diet once your body has adjusted.

Try to avoid refined foods, as most of the natural goodness has been stripped from them. Instead, attempt to use unrefined and whole grain foods where starches are concerned. Replace refined sugars with natural sweeteners such as honey, stevia, and agave. Instead of processed fruit and vegetables in cans, try to consume fresh fruit and vegetables as much as possible. If you choose to eat dried fruits, try and avoid those that have additional sugar added in the preservation process.

You may want to consider staying away from dairy. Most people are not physically able to digest dairy. This is the reason why incidences of allergic reactions to milk and milk-related products are so high. In addition to allergic reactions, milk has a long-term negative impact on your body. It has been said to increase the likelihood of developing diseases such as osteoporosis, cancer, and insulin-dependent diabetes (Ashby, 2002.)

If you need to find a substitute for milk in your diet and recipes, use one of the plant-based milk alternatives that are available on the market. These include coconut milk, almond milk, oat milk, and others.

You may want to consider removing wheat from your diet. Like milk, regular wheat causes an allergic reaction in most people due to a genetic inability to digest it. A blocked nose, phlegm, and inflammation are common reactions to the reintroduction of wheat into the body. If you insist on having baked goods, consider finding wheat alternatives such as coconut flour, almond flour, and other healthier options.

Consider reducing or eliminating the intake of meat from your diet. It may be beneficial for you to follow a pescatarian or flexitarian eating plan. However, when doing so, remember to substitute all milk and dairy products with plant-based alternatives.

Overall, attempt to avoid foods that were considered dull foods by the ancient Kemetics due to the fact that they caused aggressive behavior, disease, and negative thoughts. These foods include fermented and overripe foods, processed and refined foods, and alcohol. These foods have been said to result in dullness of mind, anger, greed, and hatred. People who consume these foods have been said to lose their ability to implement reason. Tobacco consumption was also considered to contribute to the aforementioned negative consequences.

Foods that were described as agitating are also beneficial to avoid. These are foods such as meat, coffee, and spicy or sour foods. These foods have been said to cause one to be restless and lack focus due to being easily distracted.

FASTING

Inhabitants of Kemet fasted for a period of three consecutive days every month. The purpose of fasting was to prevent the onset of disease in the form of *Ukhedu*—the source of disease that exists in the intestines. This is brought about through the build-up of food in the bowels, which needs to be removed through fasting. Thus, the ancient Egyptians usually accompanied their fasting period with the use of an enema to further clear out the intestines.

Fasting enables your body to rid itself of toxins and reduces the strain on your digestive system. Energy that would have been used to digest food is made available for use in mental and spiritual activities, such as meditation and prayer. During the course of fasting, the body diverts energy toward repairing damaged cells. During that period of time, disease-causing inflammation is reduced, and the body burns excess fat. Long-term positive effects of fasting include hormonal changes that impact gene expression. The epigenetic effects of changes in gene expression will benefit both you and future generations.

In pursuit of three days of total fasting that was practiced in ancient Kemet, there are three different types of fasting methods that are popular in modern times that you can employ in preparation.

One such method is intermittent fasting. This is the

method whereby you regularly eat only within a certain window of time during a 24-hour period. Such an eating window can consist of anything from five to eight hours of the day. If you want to practice intermittent fasting, you may start off by having a late breakfast or skip breakfast and have an early lunch. You can then have an early supper, allowing you to enter your fasting window during the course of the evening until mid-morning of the following day. During the fasting window, you can consume drinks such as water, herbal teas, and natural juices. Avoid the consumption of alcohol and caffeinated beverages.

Another method involves cutting meat out totally from the diet and eating only vegetables. This is a good method to follow if you need to wean yourself from meat as you move toward a Kemetic diet. If you are already vegetarian, consider using a fruit-only diet. This is a useful way to cleanse your body.

As somebody who is moving toward the Kemetic goal of fasting three days a month, you can start by fasting for a few hours each day before moving to intermittent fasting. Once your body has become accustomed to the concept of only eating during a short time frame, you can intensify the time period to one fasting day per month. Once you are used to this, you can fast for one day a week. Over time, you can increase this so that you are fasting for three consecutive days each month, as they did in ancient Kemet.

During your period of fasting, drinking liquids will help to flush toxins out of your body. Liquids consumed can include water, nut juices, herbal teas, and freshly squeezed juices made from both fruit and vegetables. Ingredients can include spinach, kale, cabbage, lettuce, carrots, oranges, apples, cucumbers, and other fruit and vegetables that can be consumed in their raw form.

Try to refrain from going on a water-only fast until you have been engaging in regular fasting activities for a period of one to two years. By this time, your body will have been cleansed from years of built-up *Ukhedu* toxins in your system, giving you the capacity to handle such a fast.

Be gentle with your body while you are fasting. Do not physically over-exert yourself. Rather, perform activities that are more geared toward rest and allow yourself to be directed by your body with regard to the activities you undertake.

When breaking your fast, try to limit your intake of starches or avoid them altogether on the first day. Your body needs a gentle introduction to food at this point. Starch could quickly clog up your digestive system as it is not water-soluble. As always, you must take responsibility for your own actions and dietary choices and do your own research and due diligence, no matter which route you choose to take.

SHU

⚜ 6 ⚜
KEMETIC SPIRIT GUIDES, CHAKRA SECRETS, AND CALLING UPON STRENGTH AND WISDOM

We are all surrounded by spirit guides. These are beings that exist in the spiritual realm. Their assistance makes it easier for you to access the forces of nature. By partnering with your spirit guides, you can achieve your desires, as they are the ones that will engage with the forces of nature that make all things possible. By engaging with them, you access their capacity to act as intermediaries for you in achieving your goals. Spiritual guides are in our lives to assist us through life by providing protection, comfort, and guidance with our daily activities.

ANCESTORS

These spirit guides can take different forms. One, is in the form of ancestors. These are individuals in or close to your family line. They tend to be individuals who lived an exemplary life and have made themselves available to assist the living in doing the same.

You may honor your ancestors by building an ancestral altar. This is a place set aside to communicate and engage with them.

SETTING UP AN ALTAR

To set up an altar, you may use a small table, which should be used only for this purpose. To invite the ancestors in, you can cover the table with a white tablecloth or put white seashells around the borders of the table. You can then adorn the table with photos of your ancestors—those loved ones who have left earth.

To start your engagement, pray that God (or whomever god or goddess you'd like) guides your ancestors and provides them with strength and wisdom. In this way, when you call upon them, they will have the necessary spiritual tools to provide you with the assistance that you need.

You can place a small white candle on an altar. This can be the size of a birthday candle. While it is lit, tell your ancestors that you appreciate what they did for you while they were still alive. Let them know about your life, how it is going, and any challenges that you may be facing. Ask them for guidance and assistance in addressing these challenges. In exchange for the assistance that you expect to receive from them, make an offering. The offering does not just serve to communicate with your ancestors further. It also serves as a means of balancing the energy exchange between yourself and them. As you receive their assistance with your challenges, you must give something in return. This is in accordance with the laws of Ma'at. You can give them an offering of something that they will appreciate or that they appreciated while they were alive on earth. This can be in the form of the burning of incense or the placement of something to consume. You can offer a beverage in the form of a cup of strong black coffee, a glass of alcohol—if they enjoyed this during their lifetime—or a cup of aromatic herbal tea. You can also offer your ancestors a plate of their favorite foods. After making your requests alongside your offering, thank your ancestors for their help and leave the candle to burn down by itself.

After you have offered the food and beverage, you can allow the beverage to evaporate. However, you may want to remove the plate of food the following day so that it does not become stale on the altar. When disposing of the plate of food, pray over your bin before depositing the food in it. You can also dispose of it by composting it.

Following your communication with your ancestors at the altar, be prepared for them to respond. They will provide you with direction on the steps you should take. This can occur in the form of moments of insight, hunches, and dreams that you have following your offering to them.

GODS AND GODDESSES AS SPIRIT GUIDES

As you continue your journey into Kemetic spirituality, you may become aware of various gods and goddesses making their presence known in your life. They are there to assist you in your spiritual journey by providing you with prompts on actions to take and choices to make. They may have been guiding your life journey all along, but due to a lack of awareness, you may not have recognized evidence of their existence. Such evidence may be subtle and come in the form of dreams or interactions involving some of the animals that the principles manifest as. You may now recall a time in your life that was particularly challenging. It could be that during that season, you experienced coincidences involving lions, cats, or jackals, among other animals. Your challenging situation may have been mysteriously resolved. In hindsight, you can now be aware that this was perhaps Sekhmet, Bastet, or Anubis making their presence known to you. The mysterious resolution of your challenge was perhaps due to their intervention.

The presence of the gods and goddesses can also be felt during Sekhem healing sessions. These healing sessions call upon spiritual energy; therefore, it is normal for the individual's spirit guide to reveal themselves during the healing session. This will occur in the form of mental pictures or the awareness of the presence of that god or goddess. These images or sensations can be felt either by the healer or by the person undertaking the session.

When this happens, and you are aware that one of the gods or goddesses is your spirit guide, you can greatly benefit from this knowledge. You can now ask for their direct intervention in certain issues. You can make offerings to them in the same manner as you do for your ancestors.

Taking time out to meditate and focus on the principle in question as you do so will open the way for you to receive particular guidance. Sometimes the god or goddess as a spirit guide only makes an appearance in your life for a particular purpose. At other times, they are your constant companion, guiding you through life.

Here are some of the gods and goddesses that you may encounter. Pay attention to your visions, dreams, and intuition. Also, be aware of any particular need that you have at the moment. The gods and goddesses may be called upon to intervene in a particular area that is under their protection.

Anubis, or Anpu, is the jackal-headed god of the afterlife, healing, and a guide to the lost. Anubis comes to help us with death and rebirth, often as part of the emotional, psychological, or spiritual journey.

Bastet is the cat goddess of love, fire, music, fertility, and magic. She is a protector of households who wards off evil spirits and disease.

Het-Heru, or Hathor, is a beautiful goddess bearing bull's horns and a solar disk on her head. She also manifests as a goose, lion, or cat. Goddess of cosmetics and the sky, she is known to be a protector of women. She brings pleasure, love, fertility, beauty, and music into the lives of those she touches. She is the goddess of motherhood, whose other duty is to welcome dead spirits into the afterlife. She is a less ferocious manifestation of Sekhmet. As a spirit guide, Hathor inspires gratitude and diplomacy with foreign nations and is the protector of the heavenly Nile river.

Sekhmet is the lion-headed goddess who wears a solar

disk combined with a uraeus serpent as a crown. Both ferocious and nurturing, she is a healer to the diseased and a
fierce protector of the innocent. She fiercely defends the
principles of Ma'at and will step in if you have been treated
unfairly.

CHAKRAS

Chakras are energy focal points that are found along the
spinal cord. These chakras are constantly spinning. The
impact of this is that your sense of balance is affected by the
rate at which these focal points spin. When your balance is
impacted by one of these chakras spinning slower or faster
than the others, the effect can be emotional, physical, or
mental.

There are seven main chakra points, all vibrating to
their own color. Each point is associated with a different
god or goddess on the Kemetic tree of life. These chakra
points are also aligned with different parts of the body
according to their location on the spinal column. If you have
a challenge in a particular area of your body, call upon the
gods and goddesses that govern that part of your body for
healing. Below is a basic overview of the chakra points and
an indication of which deities govern them.

1. The Root Chakra, or The Khab, is governed by
   the lower part of Geb and is associated with the
   hips, bladder, lower limbs, and groin. It is

located at the base of the spine. The color associated with the root chakra is red.

2. The Sacral Chakra, or The Khaibit, is governed by the upper part of Geb and is associated with the womb and urinary tract, and our emotions and animal senses. It is located just below your belly button. The color associated with the sacral chakra is orange.

3. The Solar Plexus Chakra, or The Sahu, is governed by Het-Heru—also known as Hathor, Sebek, and Auset. It is associated with the lungs, stomach, intestines, liver, and blood pressure. It is located above the belly button. The color associated with the solar plexus chakra is yellow.

4. The Heart Chakra, or The Ab, is governed by Ma'at, Herekuti, and Heru. It is associated with the upper back and the heart. It is located in the chest. The colors associated with the heart chakra are green and pink.

5. The Throat Chakra, or The Shekem, is governed by Sekhert and is associated with the thyroid, nose, and throat. It is located in the throat. The color associated with the throat chakra is blue.

6. The Third Eye Chakra, or The Khu, is governed by Tehuti and is associated with the eyes and ears. It is located between the eyes and

the eyebrows. The color associated with the third eye chakra is violet.

7. The Crown Chakra, or The Ba, is governed by Ausar and is associated with the nervous system, memory, and a sense of balance. It is located at the top of the head. The color associated with the crown chakra is white.

Further details about the chakra points will be provided in the chapter on Kemetic energy healing.

AURAS

Each of us radiates the energy frequency that we are operating on. This energy surrounds our bodies in the form of an electromagnetic field. Your field of energy can be sensed by other people as their own energy fields come into contact with yours. When they sense your energy field, they can react to it. The reaction is dependent on how your energy engages with their aura. From this experience, people will describe how they received good vibes or bad vibes from a person.

When other people sense your energy field, what they are picking up on is your aura. The aura exists in different layers, each a different color in alignment with your chakras and the amount of energy being radiated from each chakra. This, in turn, is influenced by your current experiences and the emotions that accompany them.

There are some people who have the capacity to see

auras and will be able to tell which aura is out of alignment just by looking at the colors emanating from your body. Auras are measurable and can even be photographed when special equipment is used. This equipment is a useful tool when determining whether there has been a change in the aura and in the balancing of chakras before and after an energy healing session.

SPIRITUAL BATHS

As we interact with other people's vibes or auras, an energy exchange takes place, and we walk away from interactions with others having been somewhat affected by them. If we constantly engage with individuals who have low energy, our energy frequency will eventually be affected. This leaves us feeling low or in a negative mood. The way to relieve ourselves from these negative moods is to cleanse our energy frequencies. A spiritual bath is one of the most effective methods that require the least amount of skill to engage in.

At the bare minimum, a spiritual bath requires a large enough bowl to put your feet into without them touching each other, coupled with your prayers and intention. Your intention should be to draw the negative energy out of your body and into the water. After a period of between 10 to 15 minutes with your feet in the water, you can take your feet out and flush the water down the toilet. Rinse the bowl out with fresh water.

To be more effective, you can add cleansing minerals to

your water in the form of rock salt, pure sea salt, or even seawater.

Your intention to cleanse your entire body can be fulfilled by taking a bath in water that has cleansing properties added to it. Combine this with a prayerful intention for spiritual cleansing. If you are not able to immerse your body fully in such water, you can pour some over you in the shower.

To increase the capacity of the water to draw out negative energy from your aura, you may add some of the following items: rock salt (refrain from using refined table salt), herbs, natural scents, tea bags, stones, and crystals. Always bless your water before taking the spiritual bath, as the intention behind the bath or shower is what increases its effectiveness.

Herbs that are effective include basil and lavender.

THOTH

✤ 7 ✤
FORGOTTEN EGYPTIAN ENERGY HEALING SECRETS AND POWERFUL MODERN TECHNIQUES

O ur bodies are conductors of energy. Not only do they conduct energy, but they contain within them the energy necessary for our survival. This energy is maintained in the energy centers, which are often referred to as chakras. The word *chakra* means "wheel of light" in the Sanskrit language of India. This has been adopted throughout the world as a way of referring to these energy centers.

The chakras have minor and major instances in the human body. The major chakras are located along the spinal cord, while minor chakras are located in different organs as well as at certain points that are in proximity to the body, such as just above the head. When seen by those who have the capacity to see energy, either through special abilities or through the use of tools, the chakras are seen as spinning wheels of light energy. It is these different-colored balls of light that have given rise to their name.

The basis of energy healing is the balancing of the main chakras, or energy centers, in the body. When the chakras are aligned, energy is able to flow freely between them. They are all in balance with each other, with none of them being more dominant or submissive than the others. A healthy body is one that is in alignment with the energy of the universe, and this is what we should all strive for. When the body is not aligned, energy healing is done in order to realign the chakras. Energy healing is achieved by accessing the energy force of the universe and bringing your body into alignment with it through techniques that cleanse your aura. When your chakras are clear, your aura is clear too. This impacts both your physical and emotional well-being. A clear aura enables energy to be easily channeled through your body. You will be able to enjoy good health and clarity of mind. However, if any of your energy centers are blocked, this may show up in disease or a psychological disorder in the area corresponding to that chakra. Often, to identify which of your chakras is blocked, you need only work back from the symptoms that your body presents. Therefore, it is important to have an understanding of the energy centers and how these impact your overall health. Once you have an awareness of these, you can use energy healing techniques to heal your body. Continuous sessions will ensure that your body stays in alignment with positive energy vibrations to enable continuous health.

To build your awareness of how energy affects your body, let us look at the seven chakras and what these represent. This will be followed by a discussion on the methods used by practitioners of Egyptian energy healing to balance these energy centers. This will also include a look at the Kemetic tree of life and how this aligns with the seven chakras and Kemetic spirituality.

In looking at the tree of life, we recognize the role that various gods and goddesses have to play in the healing journey—in particular, Sekhmet, Thoth, and Auset, who were the gods associated with the priests and priestesses of the healing temples. These priests and priestesses were tasked with both the spiritual and physical well-being of those who sought their assistance. They, in turn, would look for guidance from these gods and goddesses to identify and resolve their ailments.

HEALING FOR MA'AT

We will also examine the various tools and techniques that can be used to balance energy in the body. Remember that good health is to have balance in body, soul, and mind. While you can read books and attend inspirational lectures to sustain a healthy mind, your body and soul are directly impacted by the energy you come in contact with daily. Every time you interact with people physically, you engage with their energy. The negative interaction they may have had before coming to meet with you will remain in their energy body if they have not dealt with it prior to your meeting. When you meet with them, that energy will affect you as you will absorb it. You may walk away feeling low in spirits without knowing why you feel that way. When you are part of a crowd, such as a theater full of people, you will be affected as well. In fact, the entire crowd could infect each other with the same energy. That is why you are uplifted when you pass by a person who is smiling to themselves after hearing some good news they just received. You will notice that you may be inspired to smile, too, even if the person is not smiling at you. Most people are instinctively drawn to that positive energy because they also want to exist within a positive vibrational space. On the other hand, as much as witnessing positive energy in others can uplift you, exposure to their negative energy can also impact you. People who are close to or part of an angry crowd can often form a mob and take up action for a cause that they do not believe in. This happens because they get caught up in the energy of the crowd. For this reason, it is important whom we associate with as their energy will affect us. In instances where we do not have a choice, we need to find ways to cleanse our chakras daily if possible. This will ensure that you live your life in the most balanced way possible. Therefore, this chapter is presented to you with a view toward helping you access the right tools to keep your chakras balanced and to help you live a balanced life. A balanced life is one that is in alignment with the principles of Ma'at and, therefore, essential to your spiritual journey. By using the tools presented here, you can live in Ma'at despite the impact of your current circumstances, surroundings, or daily interactions.

THE CHAKRA SYSTEM

The human body contains seven main chakras. They are found at various locations along the spinal column and are represented by different colors. These chakras also relate to different physical, emotional, and psychological aspects of well-being. Therefore, if one chakra is out of balance in your life, it will be reflected in an imbalance of the associated physical, emotional, and psychological aspects of your life. We are going to briefly go through the 7 main chakras from the bottom to the top. This will provide you with an understanding of what these are and the aspects of the body that they relate to. They will be presented to you in the same order that you will take when ascending the tree of life.

In ancient Egypt, the chakras were seen as souls of Ra, or "Sephek Ba Ra." Our focus here will be on the chakras represented by each sphere on the tree of life. We will also look at the spiritual purpose that each chakra fulfills in relation to its position on the tree of life.

This will show you why being in spiritual alignment through the balancing of chakras provides you with the means of overcoming daily challenges and living an increasingly godly life.

Root Chakra, The Khab

Red is the color associated with the root chakra, which is located at the base of the spine.

The root chakra is responsible for enabling you to feel safe and secure, as it allows you to be grounded in reality.

On the tree of life, this chakra aligns with sphere 10. In this instance, it relates to the lower half of Geb. This relates to the physical aspects of the body and the ability to move. It is connected to our physical body. The Khab is also considered to house the unconscious spiritual body. It relates to our sensual nature.

An imbalance in the root chakra is reflected by feelings of anxiety, panic, and insecurity. This imbalance can result in a victim mentality. It can also show up in a scarcity mindset that is evidenced by hoarding. Physical ailments of the root chakra are found in the groin, bladder, lower limbs, and hips.

SACRAL CHAKRA, *The Khaibit*

Orange is the color of the sacral chakra. This chakra is located in your abdomen, about two inches below your belly button.

The sacral chakra is responsible for your sense of pleasure and well-being, including your sexuality.

On the tree of life, this chakra aligns with sphere ten. This time, it relates to the upper half of Geb, pertaining to emotions and our animal senses. This is our shadow self, which is ruled by the senses. This chakra relates to sensuality and creativity.

An imbalance in the sacral chakra is reflected by a physical and emotional sense of separation. You may experience difficulty connecting with others. Physical ailments characterized by such a blockage include fertility challenges, such as irregular menstruation, urinary problems, and gynecological issues. You may also experience back pain and constipation.

SOLAR PLEXUS CHAKRA, *The Sahu*

The solar plexus chakra is denoted by yellow.

Located in the upper abdomen, the solar plexus chakra is responsible for feelings of self-control and confidence. This is the body's center for personal power.

On the tree of life, this chakra aligns with spheres seven, eight, and nine. Sphere seven is Het-Heru, the seat of sexual energy, the Kundalini, and the Solar Forces. Sphere eight is Sebek, who represents intellect and logic as well as communication and belief. Sphere nine is Auset, the goddess who represents our personality. This is made up of our memory, the soul, and what we learn through our journey. The ability to nurture and be devoted serves to add new aspects to our ever-developing personality. This is the location of the spiritual energy body. It transports our vital force to heaven after we die.

An imbalance in the solar plexus chakra is seen in gut and stomach issues, such as indigestion. Other physical ailments you could experience are high blood pressure and liver problems. Such an imbalance could result in emotional challenges such as low self-esteem and self-doubt.

. . .

Heart Chakra, The Ab

The center for love and feelings of empathy, the heart chakra is denoted by the colors green and pink.

The heart chakra is responsible for love, empathy, forgiveness, and compassion.

On the tree of life, this chakra aligns with spheres four, five, and six. From these, we see that four is Ma'at, who governs harmony, truth, and divine law. This ideal is supported by sphere five, Heru-Khuti, who enforces divine law. Sphere six is Heru, who represents the human will that determines the outcomes of our decision-making process and the ability to overcome our lower selves. The Ab is a gateway between the divine and the mundane aspects within ourselves. It represents the seat of intellect and conscience.

An imbalance in the heart chakra is reflected by upper back pain, heart diseases, depression, anxiety, and chronic fatigue.

Throat Chakra, The Shekem

Located in your throat, at the center of the larynx, this chakra is represented by the color blue.

The throat chakra is responsible for communication. The highest form of this occurs when you are speaking your authentic truth.

On the tree of life, this chakra aligns with sphere three, which relates to the power of creation through the use of words. This is the location of our divine powers and life energy. It enables us to express our creativity and power.

An imbalance in the throat chakra is reflected by cold symptoms, throat problems, a thyroid imbalance, and a stiff neck.

THIRD EYE CHAKRA, *The Khu*

Located between your eyebrows and your eyes, the third eye chakra is associated with the color purple or indigo.

The third eye chakra is responsible for dreaming and intuition.

On the tree of life, this chakra aligns with sphere two, which relates to the omniscience of God. This is the location of the higher self or transfigured self. It is from here that our spirit enters the afterlife when we die. The Khu allows us to receive messages from the spiritual realm in our current state of being alive on earth.

An imbalance in the third eye chakra is reflected in challenges with your ears or eyes. You may also experience hormonal imbalance, sleep paralysis, or learning disabilities.

CROWN CHAKRA, *The Ba*

The crown chakra is represented by white or violet.

The crown chakra is responsible for your ability to connect to higher intelligence and the spiritual realm.

On the tree of life, this chakra aligns with sphere one,

which is related to our true selves as the manifestation of god in the world. This chakra relates to all that is supernatural and divine. The Ba also represents those aspects within us that are not physical.

An imbalance in the third eye chakra is reflected by a nervous system imbalance and problems such as memory loss, dizziness, problems with vision, and challenges with cognition.

ENERGY HEALING TECHNIQUES

When your chakras are in alignment, they are in a state of Ma'at, which is to say that they are in balance. However, there are many events and interactions that take place during the course of our daily lives. Some of the routines from these can challenge our state of Ma'at and throw us out of alignment. These events tend to affect the particular chakra that they come in contact with. For example, when you are in a situation where you are unable to speak your truth, it will affect your throat chakra. Such a situation could arise in the kind of work environment where communicating your creative ideas is stifled, like in the kind of environment where management insists that the same old methods should be used to approach tasks, even if the technology exists for better outcomes. Being strongly discouraged from expressing your ideas on how to resolve old problems in a new manner could leave you with a sore throat from a blocked throat chakra.

This is a real-world example of how failure to bring

alignment to your chakras on a continuous basis can end up making you feel uneasy or manifest a diseased body. The following techniques were used in ancient Kemet and are being embraced once again in modern times as a means to address bodily imbalances.

PRAYERS AND AFFIRMATIONS

One way of bringing healing energy into your body is through the use of positive words. The power of words as a strong vibrational force with the capacity to create the universe has been increasingly recognized by globally acclaimed teachers like Bob Proctor of "Born Rich." Therefore, one method that you can use is to speak life into your energy centers. This enables them to align with the truth that you are speaking to them rather than with any dis-ease that they may have encountered. You can do this for all your chakras as a daily practice, or you can focus on a single chakra when you feel it has become out of balance for its purpose. You can use the symptoms that your body presents combined with knowledge of each chakra. This way, you can identify the areas that need special attention. The following are suggested affirmations that can be used for each of your chakras. You may change these or add to them in accordance with what works for your particular situation and symptoms.

AFFIRMATIONS FOR THE ROOT CHAKRA, The Khab

- I live in abundance and always receive provision.
- I am grateful for the life I live.
- I am confident.
- I am respected by all who know me.
- I am grounded in my sense of belonging.

AFFIRMATIONS FOR THE SACRAL CHAKRA, The Khaibit

- Mutual appreciation and respect are central to all my relationships.
- My loved ones can trust me, and I can trust them.
- I am constantly inspired to act on new ideas.
- I express my creativity in many different ways.
- I take full responsibility for my happiness and nurture myself emotionally.

AFFIRMATIONS for The Solar Plexus Chakra, The Sahu

- I live in alignment with my divine purpose.
- I am confident that I am always worthy.
- I use past mistakes as stepping stones to propel me forward.
- I am confident, powerful, and strong.
- I am motivated to face challenges.

AFFIRMATIONS FOR THE HEART CHAKRA, The Ab

- I am surrounded by love everywhere I go.
- I am full of love and attract people who are full of love.
- I love myself fully.
- I welcome love and give it the attention it deserves.
- I deserve to be loved.

AFFIRMATIONS FOR THE THROAT CHAKRA, The Shekem

- I am a good listener who is patient and attentive.
- I am good at communicating my ideas in a calm and considerate way.

- I enjoy vibrant and intelligent conversations.
- Success and prosperity are regular themes in my speech.
- I speak confidently and clearly.

Affirmations for The Third Eye Chakra, The Khu

- I am divinely guided toward my higher purpose.
- I am open to new experiences.
- I always trust my intuition.
- I am a big-picture thinker who acts with wisdom and intuition.
- I am connected to the divine.

Affirmations for The Crown Chakra, The Ba

- I am an extension of loving, divine energy.
- I am spiritual, presently living as a human.
- I receive new ideas from the universe.
- As higher powers guide me, they add to my inner wisdom.
- I embrace the present moment and live in the now.

LAYING OF HANDS

You can augment your affirmations by laying your hands over the area relating to the chakra that you are focusing on. You may place your hands side by side over the physical location on the body where the chakra is found. You may also choose to only use your dominant hand over the area. This is something you can do while lying on your back.

What is more effective is to place the hands on opposite sides of the body so that they enclose the affected area. This requires a bit of dexterity for areas like the chest, as one hand will be in front of your chest, and the other hand will be on your back in the corresponding area. Placing your hands in these positions requires you to stand or to be in a seated position, with your feet firmly on the ground and your back straight. From this position, the method that you would use when saying words of affirmation for your sacral chakra would require you to place your right hand just below your belly button. At the same time, you would place your left hand on your lower back. In this way, the energy will flow from both your hands through your body into the affected chakra. You can employ this method when you are praying for somebody else as well. To enhance your ability to access universal energy while doing the chakra balancing exercises, call upon your spirit guides to direct you toward the chakras that need the most attention. Take a deep breath and remain calm as you visualize your spirit guide placing their hand on top of yours to perform the healing exercise through you as you do it.

USE OF HEALING RODS

Many of the statues that were found in ancient temples in Kemet depicted the gods and goddesses holding cylinders in their hands. It was only in the last century that the truth about these cylinders came to light. This was after a Zoroastrian yoga school revealed an ancient text in the 1920s. This text was used by Russian scientists in the 1990s to recreate the rods. The rods were then studied by the Russian Academy of Sciences over a period of ten years. The result of their intensive study was the discovery that the rods used similar processes to heal the body as acupuncture and reiki. They determined that the rods were composed of specific metals and crystals, which enable healing to occur faster in the body when they are correctly used. The rods are also used for manifestation, physical balancing, and ascension.

Therefore, it was only in recent times that it was determined that what these statues were, in fact, holding were healing rods. These rods kept them in a constant state of balance and alignment due to the mineral composition of the rods.

There are ten different types of rods. Each set of rods is specific to the energy capacity of different people in accordance with the frequency and vibration that they align with. Holding a set of rods for just five minutes opens the meridians and balances the chakras, enabling energy to flow easily throughout the body. It is estimated that the benefit you will experience within those five minutes would require a 30-minute acupuncture session to achieve.

A set of rods comprises a copper or gold sun rod and a zinc or silver moon rod. The sun rod contains masculine ying energy, while the moon rod contains feminine yang energy.

When used by an individual to attain balance, the sun rod is placed in the right hand, and the moon rod is placed in the left hand. The result is that restorative energy flows through the body of the person holding the rods.

When used by a practitioner such as a reiki healer, the rods can be directed toward the patient to enable the energy healing session to occur. While the practitioner is moving the rods over the patient, another set of rods can be held in the patient's hands to increase the energy flow. The session may also take place with only the practitioner carrying the healing rods.

The rods can be used daily for a period of between 10 to 20 minutes. The positive effect of holding these rods to channel energy through your body has been proven. Aside from increasing feelings of being centered and grounded, the use of the rods has the following benefits:

- They alleviate symptoms of chronic fatigue and exhaustion.
- They improve sleep quality and resolve insomnia.
- They enhance mental clarity for meditation by stimulating mental and physical energy.
- They regulate the nervous system, resulting in the removal of symptoms of over-agitation,

obsessive-compulsive movements, and nervous tics.

- They assist with the growth and function of nerves.
- They regulate early-stage high blood pressure and its associated cardiovascular diseases. This includes problems such as arteriosclerosis and heart arrhythmia.
- They boost the nervous system.
- They remove symptoms of stress and depression from the body.
- They have a positive impact on the endocrine system.
- They improve the condition of the excretory system. This reduces the likelihood of the occurrence of kidney infections, irritable bowel syndrome, and bladder infections.

With all the positive effects of the rods, you need to be aware that there are circumstances in which they should not be used. Those who should not use the rods include the following people:

- Those who are under the influence of recreational drugs
- Children
- Those who make use of pacemakers
- Those who are pregnant

- Those with low blood pressure
- Those with serious mental health challenges such as schizophrenia

The use of healing rods has been combined with other healing methods, such as Reiki and Sekhem healing, to transfer the benefits of the power of the rods to an ill person. Both these methods access universal energy to transfer its benefits to a patient. When used in conjunction with the healing rods, the effects of the energy transfer are amplified. The rods can also be used by practitioners to replenish their own energy between sessions with different clients.

TAPPING ENERGY MERIDIAN POINTS

The ancient Egyptians had a solid understanding of energy within the body. Although this technique didn't sprout from their culture directly and has only been introduced in recent years, it nonetheless remains an incredibly powerful tool for providing those on a spiritual path with accelerated inner and personal growth, which is why it is mentioned here.

In using the energy tapping technique to clear energetic blockages and traumas, it will become a great deal easier to live by the laws of Ma'at, be at one with nature, and skyrocket your spiritual growth. It is an easy technique you can do from literally anywhere, and it requires no special tools or equipment.

Most of us live in a stressful environment, which can be made worse by a lack of control and uncertainty. This can give rise to feelings of anxiety about a lot of factors, especially when we watch the news, as we cannot control the narrative. Being in stressful conditions gives rise to adrenaline, the fight or flight hormone that our bodies release when preparing their primitive response to danger. However, without an outlet for these hormones and with continued negative stimulation from the environment, we can be in danger of building up more stress in our bodies.

To counteract the effects of negative emotions, you can directly tap into your body's energy meridians (energy channels) to reduce the amount of adrenaline and cortisol in your body. This technique works in a way similar to acupuncture and acupressure but consists of tapping with your hand on different points on your head, face, and body, in tandem with spoken (or even silent) affirmations. It works by focusing on various energy meridian areas that connect to different organs in your body. The organs that the tapping exercises connect to hold emotions in your body, such as anger, stress, anxiety, or sadness. It works to process emotions and reduce levels of hormonal build-up in the body. You also reduce the impact that stress has on the rest of your body. Simply put, you are able to access the subconscious mind, remove traumas, limiting beliefs, and what no longer serves you. You can then replace this obsolete programming with an updated way of operating in the world that serves you better and aligns with your higher purpose. People have even used this technique to eradicate their fear of spiders, flying, driving, and theme park rides, among others. It really is that easy to do, and there are no limits to the subjects it can clear.

TAPPING POINTS

There are nine tapping points that have been identified.

1. The first tapping point is the karate chop point. It is abbreviated KC. This is located on the side of each hand. To locate it, find the fleshy part of the hand that is just below the pinky finger and above the wrist. This point connects to the small intestine. It assists with releasing grief, moving forward, and finding joy in the present moment.

2. The second tapping point is the eyebrow. It is abbreviated EB. To locate this point, trace your finger around the bone that outlines your eye socket. The point where this bone meets your eyebrows is where you should tap. This point connects to the bladder. It eases trauma, sadness, and feelings of being hurt while enabling emotional healing and inner peace.

3. The third tapping point is the side of the eye. It is abbreviated SE. It is located on the bone next to where your upper and lower eyelids meet.

This point connects to the gallbladder. Tapping this point promotes clarity and compassion while releasing anger and resentment.

4. The fourth tapping point is under the eye. It is abbreviated UE. For both eyes, it is located in the middle of the bone directly below your eye. This point connects to the stomach. It releases feelings of fear and anxiety while enabling calmness, contentment, and a sense of safety.

5. The fifth tapping point is under the nose. It is abbreviated UN. It is located in the area below your nose and above your top lip. It connects to the Governing Vessel meridian point. Tapping on this point will help ease feelings of powerlessness, shame, grief, embarrassment, and fear of failure while promoting self-acceptance, self-empowerment, and compassion.

6. The sixth tapping point is the chin point. It is abbreviated CP. It is located at the indentation under your lower lip, at the top of the chin area. This point connects with the Central meridian and enhances your capacity for self-acceptance, confidence, certainty, clarity, and security.

7. The seventh tapping point is the collarbone. It is abbreviated CB. If you move your finger along your collarbone, you will find a spot where it makes a slight indentation before it rises up to

create the top of the V shape that meets the sternum. At this indentation point, move your fingers down until you can feel the top of the bone from your first rib. In between the collar bone and the rib point is the CB meridian point. It is located on both the left and right sides of your body. This point connects to the kidneys. It helps you move forward, reducing feelings of being stuck, and boosts confidence and clarity.

8. The eighth tapping point is the underarm. It is abbreviated UA. It is located about four inches below the armpit. This point connects to the spleen. It will help you cope with guilt, worry, obsession, indecision, and criticism.

9. The ninth tapping point is the top of the head point. It is abbreviated TOH. It is located at the very center of the top of your head if you were to look down at it from above. This point connects to multiple energy points and to the crown chakra. It helps with spiritual connection, clarity, intuition, and wisdom.

To engage in the tapping technique:

1. Find a quiet place where you are not distracted by another activity while you go through the exercise.

2. Close your eyes and take a deep breath, then breathe out. Bring to mind the situation that

makes you feel anxious (or any other emotion or situation you would like to work on).

3. As you feel the feelings, consider the level of discomfort you feel. Assign to it a discomfort measurement of between one and ten. You can review your level of discomfort after doing a full round of tapping to determine if there has been an improvement. If there is no improvement after a single round, you can repeat the process from the beginning.

TAPPING EXERCISE

Only focus on one stressful issue per session. Tap on the meridian points, either with two fingers for the smaller areas or with four fingers to cover the larger areas. The process takes less than ten minutes.

Tap gently about seven to ten times on each of the meridian points in turn, taking a deep abdominal breath with each new meridian point. During the process, use your intuition to guide your focus. If you feel the need to tap longer on a certain meridian point, follow your inner guidance, as this will facilitate your healing process.

To start, tap on the karate chop point as you go through the affirmations below. This is the set-up stage. During this stage, you can make an affirmation that is a declaration of two statements. The first statement is to acknowledge the problem. The second statement is to accept yourself and let the problem go. Select a statement from the list below that you feel aligns with what you are feeling and repeat it as you tap each of the meridian points. The statements have been ordered according to the body's overall chakra points. You can therefore choose a statement that addresses the area in your body that is most out of alignment with the rest of your body.

Statement for your Root Chakra:

Even though I am overwhelmed, I choose to relax and feel safe knowing that Geb supports me.

Statement for your Sacral Chakra:

Even though I feel unappreciated, I choose to appreciate myself and allow Geb to guide me in expressing my emotions.

Statement for your Solar Plexus Chakra:

Even though I feel powerless, I choose to feel self-confident. I do this knowing that Auset allows my personality to shine through, while Het-Heru provides me with sexual and solar energy, and Sebek strengthens my capacity to communicate clearly.

Statement for your Heart Chakra:

Even though I am experiencing anxiety, I choose to deeply love and accept myself. Heru gives me the will to love and accept myself. This is in accordance with the divine law of Ma'at and enforced by Heru-Khuti.

Statement for your Throat Chakra:

Even though I feel insecure, I choose to express my true self. I do this through the creative power of Sekhem that resides within me.

Statement for your Third Eye Chakra:

Even though I feel uncertain, I choose to trust my intuition. I know that the intuitive power of Djehuti resides within me.

Statement for your Crown Chakra:

Even though I feel uncreative, I choose to receive

inspiration. I receive it from Ausar, who controls all of life's events.

Having completed the set-up phase, tap through each of the meridian points in turn. Think about the issue and let it go.

Closing Affirmations

Now do a second round of tapping through the meridian points while saying the following affirmations:

- It is safe to let this go.
- I am open to releasing this issue.
- I am finding peace in my body.
- I am strong, grounded, and safe in every cell of my body right now.

Once you have finished the process, think of the bothersome situation again and measure your discomfort levels on a scale of one to ten, as you did before. If your levels of discomfort have not gone down by the time you have gone through tapping on all the meridian points, repeat the exercise from the beginning.

SEKHEM ENERGY HEALING TECHNIQUE

The word *Sekhem* means "Life Energy." This energy is brought about by the intermingling of Shu and Tefnut, and it is what sustains all living things. This is the life energy that we engage with when we do Sekhem energy healing. This is done by interacting with the soul and earth chakras.

These are additional chakras to the seven major chakras which we previously examined. The soul chakra is located about 12 inches above your head, and it stores information about all your life experiences. The earth chakra is located 12 inches below your feet. It connects you to earth energy and, therefore, to nature and the Neteru.

METHOD

Sekhem Healing channels energy via these chakras through the body's energy meridians using the healer's hands and any tools they might use, such as healing rods, as a means of energy transference. The channeling of the energy through the meridians ensures that there is an equal flow of energy throughout the body. The process unblocks any chakras which may be blocked or experiencing drainage. Once all the chakras are unblocked, full vitality is maintained or will be returned to the body.

As source energy, Shekem uses energy from the star Sirius, which incidentally was referred to by ancient Egyptians as the home of departed souls. Sirius is also known as the dog star, a place which the Dogon people of West Africa referred to even before modern astronomy had created telescopes powerful enough to identify it in the cosmos. In addition to Sirius, Sekhem also channels energy from Lemuria and Orion.

If you would like to benefit from Sekhem energy healing, it is recommended that you find a practitioner who has studied this method of healing. The method uses specific techniques and symbols that are known by the practitioner to activate the different chakras and call upon the required earth and star energies.

The healer makes use of Sekhmet symbols. These are multi-dimensional symbols drawn in the air over each affected chakra. These symbols are used to guide the energy from the star systems toward the affected areas. They summon specific cosmic energies to aid in the alignment and healing process.

During the Sekhem healing session, it is normal for both the healer and the initiate being healed to experience interaction from the spiritual world. This can occur in the form of flashes of images, colors, ancestors, or some of the gods and goddesses of ancient Kemet. These all appear during the session in order to provide support and guidance during the process. For the healer, they guide them toward identifying the areas that need the most work and, there-fore, extra concentration to facilitate the healing process. For the initiate undergoing the healing process, the guid-ance is to aid in determining the direction of your life to attain balance and live in Ma'at. Following a healing session, if you did have flashes of gods and goddesses, be active in your engagement with them. Do your research to find out what these gods and goddesses stood for during the course of their lives (you will find a wealth of information within these pages). What areas of life were they in charge of, and what challenges did they have to overcome? There-after, examine your own life for similarities and see what lessons can be applied. It could be that they appeared to guide you or give you strength in a particular area of your life.

The session ends with the grounding of the patient's energy. This is done to ensure that they remain grounded after the session. Other energy healing methods that fail to integrate this step sometimes leave patients feeling dazed after the process, as their chakras remain exposed to external stimulation. To avoid this, Sekhem grounds the initiate's energy both before and after each session.

IMPACT

Due to its connection with the soul chakra, Sekhem energy healing has a beneficial effect beyond the physical body and beyond the current time. It results in a higher level of consciousness and removes energy blockages that occur as a result of past events. Therefore, in instances where people may be suffering from the prolonged effects of trauma that occurred in the past, Sekhem Healing is a good tool to use when addressing and overcoming these past traumas.

Sekhem Healing has positive emotional benefits which are discernible to those you interact with on a daily basis. Following your Sekhem Energy Healing session, those around you are likely to observe changed behavior patterns due to your increased consciousness. Therefore, the impact of a Sekhem healing session can be felt for weeks after the session has occurred. If the energy blockages that were removed have been present in the body for a long time, the session could be life-altering. The individual will be able to go through life with a different perspective and renewed energy. This can alter the projection of their life in a positive way. Because the soul carries memories from previous lifetimes, there can be instances whereby the energy being cleared may have been carried through from a previous lifetime. This residual energy will be accessible for clearing through Sekhem Healing due to the interaction with the soul chakra.

The engagement with the earth chakra and the Neteru results in increased engagement with ancestors and spirit guides. These can also come through during the session, either as momentary flashes or as a constant presence throughout the session. With Sekhem healing, it is expected for these spirit guides to be in the form of Sekhmet or Bastet. They could also be from another representative of the five pantheons that are in charge of health, such as Heka, Auset, Serket, and Ta-Bitjet.

SEKHMET

It is expected that Sekhmet energy will be felt during the healing sessions as Sekhem is the energy that was used in the healing temples. This healing energy falls into the domain of Sekhmet. Sekhmet, whose name means "the powerful one," is the goddess of healing and was the patron of the healing temples in ancient Kemet. The priests and priestesses of these temples healed both physical and spiritual ailments with the use of Sekhem energy. Sekhmet is a force that continues to guide healers today. Those who perform the roles that were performed by the priests and priestesses of the healing temples during the times of ancient Kemet will often call on Sekhmet in her various forms to guide them in their healing sessions. Sekhmet also takes on other forms, such as Bastet and Hathor. Each form that she takes on reveals a different side to her personality and brings with it different elements. As Bastet, she is a protector of individuals and of households. She shields them from diseases and evil spirits while also imbuing them with good health and fertility. As Hathor, she is the fun-loving protector of women and the goddess of motherhood.

HEALTH PANTHEONS

According to the practices of ancient Kemet, there are five pantheons that are responsible for our health. These are Sekhmet, Heka, Serket, Ta-Bitjet, and Auset. We have already discussed the lion-headed Sekhmet and her role as patron of the priests and priestesses of healing. She has the ability to bring healing and fruitfulness while retaining the capacity to bring pestilence and destruction. Therefore, her capacity to inflict pestilence gives her an understanding of illness and how to remove it, much in the way that her capacity for destruction enables her to build.

Heka

The next pantheon on our list is Heka, the god of magic and medicine. He wears a helmet with what appears to be two raised arms coming out of it. He carries a staff with two intertwined snakes. His staff has survived through time and cultures to become a modern symbol of medicine. Magic was an integral part of ancient Egypt, even beyond death. Those who did not have faith in their ability to survive the weighing of their souls against the 42 laws of Ma'at would ensure that they learned enough magic to enable them to get through the ordeal. This made Heka an important aspect of life and the afterlife, as Heka was in charge of magic. However, magic was not only important for accessing the afterlife. Heka's presence was pervasive in ancient Kemet due to magic being a part of everyday life, even for the living. The knowledge and use of the right combination of words are integral, as magic is transmitted in the form of words, both written and spoken. Even the afterlife was replete with magic. Here, those that had not managed to attain balance through the 42 laws of Ma'at would use magic spells to help them get through the test that gave entry into the afterlife.

Serket

Serket is a goddess of healing, with a special emphasis on healing from venomous bites. This emphasis is highlighted by the scorpion that she wears on her head like a crown. She is also a goddess of nature, animals, magic, and fertility. The ankh that she carries has often been identified as a symbol for the womb; therefore, it is apt that depictions of a goddess of fertility show her carrying one.

. . .

Ta-Bitjet

Ta-Bitjet is a protective goddess. Her areas of operation include bites, stings, poisons, and the hymen. Her methodology includes the use of spells and using the blood from her own hymen as an antivenom. In depictions of Ta-Bitjet, she takes on the form of a scorpion bearing the head of a woman.

AUSET

Auset, known to the Greeks as Isis, is the ultimate healer goddess. She brought her dead husband, Ausar, back to life on multiple occasions. The first time was after he was killed by his brother, and his coffin was thrown into a river. When the coffin washed ashore, a Djed tree with an attractive aroma started to grow out of it. The tree was cut down and made into a pillar for the king of Byblos. In retrieving the tree, Isis first performed the restorative task of healing the king's son. She thereafter returned with the pillar and freed her husband from within it. His brother killed him a second time. This time around, for good measure, he cut Ausar—also known as Osiris—into 14 pieces and scattered them along the Nile river. The faithful Auset gathered all the pieces she could find and assembled them for burial. Not finding the penis, she created one so that her husband could be buried whole. This was the second time that she was able to elicit life from the body of her dead husband.

Being buried whole was an important requirement for him to be accepted into the afterlife. In this whole form, her husband visited her in a dream and impregnated her. Take note of how Auset's husband was in spirit form when he impregnated her. Additionally, due to Ausar spending most of his time trying to survive his brother Set's traps, he and Auset never consummated their marriage. Therefore, when the spirit of Ausar impregnated Auset, this was the first recorded Immaculate Conception. Following this, other religions and belief systems have had similar accounts.

THESE HEALING PANTHEONS can all be called upon to aid in the healing process, especially when one is dealing with a deity's specialty, be it fertility, stings, or resurrecting aspects of your life that seem to be dead. In making your requests to them, be guided by their stories. This should be inclusive of challenges they overcame and impossible feats they engaged in during their lives on earth. Be aware that some of these pantheons existed on the earthly plane at some time—either they were born into it as Auset was, or they were sent to earth at some point in order to accomplish a specific feat as Sekhmet was. If they did not walk the earth, they engaged with ordinary individuals daily. This is the case with Heka, who was called upon to assist in all areas of life and into death as well.

As you begin your journey with Sekhem Healing, keep in mind the various aspects that make it so powerful. It provides a holistic healing experience that engages beyond the seven main chakras to include the soul and the earth chakras. In engaging these chakras, energy is derived from the cosmos and the earth. This healing method will enable you to deal with issues from both your past and your present. The intuitive guidance and insight received from Sirius energy, the ancestors, and the pantheons of Egyptian healing make this form of healing one that has the capacity to transform the trajectory of your life.

MAAT

❦ 8 ❦
DAILY KEMETIC SPIRITUAL RITUALS YOU CAN START NOW FOR FLOURISHING DIVINITY

Ma'at is the goddess of truth, harmony, law, and justice. She is often depicted in a kneeling position with one leg tucked under her body and the knee of her other leg pointing upward while the sole of the corresponding foot lays flat on the ground. Her winged arms stretch out in front of her or extend from the sides of her body.

The ostrich feather that she wears on her head is the same feather that she uses to weigh our souls when we pass from earth to heaven. Alongside her cohorts, Djehuti and Hathor, it is her actions that determine whether one's life should cease totally or if one can go on into the afterlife.

Therefore, upon waking, it is beneficial to recite the laws of Ma'at as an intention for the day. They should serve as a reminder of the things that you will refrain from. At the end of the day, recite these laws again as a means of reflecting on your day and determining whether you lived your day out as you had initially intended.

RECITING THE LAWS OF MA'AT

The Laws of Ma'at are also referred to as the 42 Principles of Ma'at. They serve as a guiding set of principles to live by. The Ten Commandments are distilled from these laws.

The 42 Laws of Ma'at are as follows:

1. I have not committed sin.
2. I have not committed robbery with violence.
3. I have not stolen.
4. I have not slain men and women.
5. I have not stolen food.
6. I have not swindled offerings.
7. I have not stolen from God.
8. I have not told lies.
9. I have not carried away food.
10. I have not cursed.
11. I have not closed my ears to truth.
12. I have not committed adultery.
13. I have not made anyone cry.
14. I have not felt sorrow without reason.
15. I have not assaulted anyone.
16. I am not deceitful.
17. I have not stolen anyone's land.
18. I have not been an eavesdropper.
19. I have not falsely accused anyone.

20. I have not been angry without reason.
21. I have not seduced anyone's wife.
22. I have not polluted myself.
23. I have not terrorized anyone.
24. I have not disobeyed the law.
25. I have not been excessively angry.
26. I have not cursed God.
27. I have not behaved with violence.
28. I have not caused disruption of peace.
29. I have not acted hastily or without thought.
30. I have not overstepped my boundaries of concern.
31. I have not exaggerated my words when speaking.
32. I have not worked evil.
33. I have not used evil thoughts, words, or deeds.
34. I have not polluted the water.
35. I have not spoken angrily or arrogantly.
36. I have not cursed anyone in thought, word, or deed.
37. I have not placed myself on a pedestal.
38. I have not stolen that which belongs to God.
39. I have not stolen from or disrespected the deceased.
40. I have not taken food from a child.
41. I have not acted with insolence.
42. I have not destroyed property belonging to God.

(AncientEgypt, n.d.)

STUDY

One way to grow your spiritual life is by taking time out to study religious texts. This can be from any of the world's major religions. The reason why studying different religions will lead you to Kemeticism is that these religions have been suspected of having Kemetic religion as their base. You can discover this for yourself if you study enough. For example, a virgin that conceived a baby via immaculate conception is a similar story to Auset, Ausar, and Heru. The world being brought into existence by sound is the story of Ra and Nefertum. The world emerging out of the water in various forms is a reflection of the BenBen rock emerging from the waters of chaos. It is thought by many that these stories have been repackaged and retold by different cultures around the world. This is why, at their base, religious stories so often point back to Kemet.

You may also benefit from studying the mythology and religion of ancient Kemet. You will have learned through the reading of this book that knowledge of the gods and goddesses is central to the Kemetic way of life. Understanding the individual stories and interactions between the deities will help you in your personal walk and in your engagements with other people. This can be done by using the knowledge of the archetypes that the deities represent and the areas of your life that these reflect. Studying the Kemetic stories alongside other religious myths will help you see the connection between the principles and beliefs of the world's major religions and those of Kemet. You may then come to understand that even though religion may have changed over time, the central principles guiding humanity have remained the same. You may realize that humanity continues to be guided by the same forces as it has always been. This should help you find a way to identify the method of worship that makes you feel most in alignment with the divine.

Having an intimate knowledge of the deities will help you identify who to call upon when faced with various challenges. By practicing theurgy, you can then take on the aspects of the deity that can help you overcome your challenge. By studying the word of God in the format in which it is available to you, you will receive knowledge and insight that you will be able to draw on daily. You will receive further guidance in the form of the religious practices and rituals that each religion maintains as central themes. These are incorporated in their teachings and involve acts such as the importance of giving as a counterbalance to the blessing of receiving. This is the law of causality, and the manner in which it is often taught is to encourage good outcomes in your life by creating the same for others.

Central to most religions is the act of prayer. This involves communicating with or calling upon the divine for assistance with achieving life goals. This is the principle of mentalism in action as you connect with the divine on a mental level. When you do so, you command the power to move atoms, the building blocks of creation, in a way that ensures the accomplishment of your goals. The more you can still your mind through the use of practices such as meditation, the greater your ability will be to engage prayer as a resource to bring about the circumstances and people that will direct you toward the next step that is needed for accomplishing your intended desire.

The existence of both good and evil in the world is depicted in multiple religions, as is the way that evil can be overcome by good. When these are personified into good and evil individuals, it is the principle of polarity being explained in a practical way that the average mind can grasp.

Therefore, religions instill within you an initial under-standing of how the deities can operate in your life. Addi-tionally, they provide a practical means of incorporating the Hermetic Laws into daily activities. These means are by way of community outreach activities, giving to the religious institution and to other institutions, and an insistence on prayer and ritual as an integral part of your life. These Hermetic Laws are an important part of living in harmony with creation and moving forward in accomplishing your targeted goals.

CLEAN EATING

Try to eat a diet that has trapped the energy of the sun in the form of green leaves and colorful foods that are rich in antibodies. This means that your diet should be sourced from natural, unrefined foods as much as possible. When you consume too many refined foods, the food is difficult to digest. Waste product from this food has a hard time being expelled from the body, causing energy blockage and potential health risks due to sacral chakra blockage. On the other hand, a diet that is sourced from plants provides the maximum amount of nutrition from your body while providing health benefits, including the ability to focus more during meditative exercise due to less energy being spent on the digestive process.

Incorporating daily spiritual rituals will enable you to stay focused on your life's purpose. Spiritual rituals can include activities such as the lighting of candles and incense, the reciting of prayers, and daily yoga and meditation. The daily reminders that occur during your prayers and your meditative practice will help you to live in alignment with the laws of Ma'at. This will occur as you put your mind in alignment with the universal consciousness and practice principles that take advantage of the Hermetic laws.

MEDITATION

Meditation is a method that is used to focus your mind. The ability to focus your mind clearly is essential to achieving your life's goals. It allows you to excel toward your desires in the midst of distracting situations. It is also a skill that enables you to tune in to the elements of divinity around you. It, therefore, enables mindfulness and responsiveness to the clues and stimuli that could be the ways in which the gods and goddesses are trying to get a message through to you. Without the focus and mindfulness that meditation brings into your life, you could have difficulty engaging in the activities that are essential to theurgy and living in a manner that continually aligns you with divinity.

Take time daily to clear your mind and allow divine wisdom to inspire you. Incorporate yoga and some chakra healing exercises into your meditative practice. These can take the form of affirmations and will ensure that your body's chakras remain cleansed. Fully aligned chakras allow you to live a balanced and healthy life as much as possible. The clearing of your mind that meditation provides creates a platform for divine inspiration to come into your life. You can only receive new messages when your mind is not filled with chaotic thoughts from your daily life. Focusing in this manner will enable you to have renewed vigor and a sense of purpose to approach your daily activities.

Meditation brings about a stillness of mind. Therefore, mindfulness is an important aspect of meditation. This can be practiced by focusing on a visual object, a sound, or a mental picture. Breathwork is also important for meditation. I will introduce you to some exercises that will incorporate some breath work as well as focus on different aspects. Each exercise will be introduced for a specific purpose and can be adjusted to suit your specific needs.

MEDITATION FOR CREATING

It is best to do this meditation when you are at the beginning or in the middle of a creative project. You can also use this as a way of beginning your day. It enables you to tap into the universal stream of creative consciousness so that you can harness it for your own creativity. It provides you with a deep understanding of how the universal process that creates big galaxies is the same process that creates dainty flowers. Once you are able to understand this concept, you can apply it in your life as a creator. This applies to all forms of creativity, whether it is a piece of artwork, music, the assembly of a chair, or a computer program. To create anything effectively, you need to access the creative energy that resides within each of us.

Before going into this simple yet effective meditative exercise, it is beneficial to learn the box breathing technique. It is called box breathing because the inhaling and exhaling breath is the same length. There is also a similar length for holding your breath on either side of these two actions. This makes the breathing process similar to drawing a square or a box with your breath. In order to engage in this technique, breathe in for four seconds, then hold your breath for four seconds. After that, exhale for four seconds and keep the exhaled breath out of your lungs for four seconds before breathing in again. Repeat the box breathing exercise before going on to the next section. Again, breathe in for four seconds, hold in for four seconds, breathe out for four seconds, and hold out for four seconds. Once you feel you have perfected the box breathing technique, you can move on to the visualizing aspect of the meditation exercise. As you visualize, continue to engage in the box breathing exercise.

Sit cross-legged on the floor with your hands relaxed

into each other on your lap. Imagine the process of creation as the Nefertum sat on the Lotus, speaking the words of creation beside Ra. As you breathe in and out, imagine this power of creation and imagine yourself participating in this process. Imagine new galaxies being born as you speak them into existence, while at the same time, a flower is formed on the stem of a plant. The flower forms a bud and grows to full bloom even as the new galaxy is being created. Breathe in and out using the box breathing technique while tapping into the power of creation that resides within you. For five minutes, maintain this aspect of gently using the box breathing technique while imagining the process of creation. If you are unable to maintain your focus for five minutes, maintain it for as long as you can while building up to it. If you can maintain your focus for more than five minutes, you are encouraged to do so, as it enhances your ability to align with the divine.

JOY MEDITATION

Find a comfortable position, whether it is sitting cross-legged on the floor or lying on your back. Close your eyes and allow your head to drop forward slightly in a relaxed pose. Breathe in deeply through your nose to allow the impact of the breath to push your stomach out. When this happens, know that you are breathing from your diaphragm. Gently exhale through your nose or through your mouth, pushing all the air out of your lungs before taking another deep inhalation. As you sit in this relaxed position, tilt your head from side to side, allowing the right side of your neck to stretch as you tilt your head to the left side. Take a deep breath in this position and exhale before tilting your head to the right side so that the left side of your neck feels stretched.

Now that you are fully relaxed, take your mind back to a moment when you laughed uncontrollably. Maybe even a time when you laughed so much that you cried. What was happening at the time? Who were you with? What inspired so much laughter? What physical activity had you been doing prior to that, if any? What did you do afterward? Can you remember the sounds, smells, and tastes from that day? When you think back to that day, what do you see in your mind's eye? Let your muscles relax as you remember these sensations and how the occasion made you feel. If you feel like smiling at the memory, go ahead and smile. If retelling a joke in the manner that it was delivered makes you laugh again, allow yourself the freedom to laugh. Feel the emotion in your chest as you continue to breathe in and out, remembering the moment. Feel the freedom of that moment when you laughed with such joy. Continue to breathe as you try and remember as much detail as you can about that moment.

Acknowledge that this particular moment will always be with you, and to feel those sensations again, all you need to do is close your eyes and remember. Knowing this, think of the moment once more, allowing yourself to feel the joy that you felt and the laughter that permeated your being. Continue to breathe as you enjoy the sensation. When you are ready to step out of the moment, raise your chin so that your face is directed straight ahead of you. Now raise your arms on either side of you until your hands are above your head. Allow your palms to touch each other gently. Inhale and exhale gently. Repeat the inhalation and exhalation process, making sure to breathe deeply. Now open your eyes and get ready to face the day with inner joy.

MEDITATION FOR MA'AT

This is a good meditation to do during those moments when you feel slightly out of control or as though you are out of sync with the world around you.

Sit with your back straight, either on the ground or on a chair. Put your hands on your knees and close your eyes. Take a deep breath, and as you exhale, think of the word 'balance.' Inhale again, and this time when you exhale, think of the word 'harmony.' Repeat the process, using the words 'peace,' 'justice,' and 'order' as the subjects you focus on with each exhalation. Balance, harmony, peace, justice, order. Spend ten minutes contemplating these words and what each of them means to you. When ten minutes have passed, spread out your arms on either side of your body. Twist your torso to the left, then twist your torso to the right. Open your eyes and come out of your contemplative state.

MEDITATION FOR RENEWAL AND COMFORT

Do this meditation when you feel drained of energy. It is a reminder that we can renew our energy levels so long as we take time to rest. Two yoga positions are used for the exercise. The first yoga position is Khepri—the scarab beetle. To get into this yoga position, kneel while you sit on your haunches. Inhale deeply and exhale. Lean forward, using your hands to steady yourself. Lower your body to the ground until your forehead is touching the floor and your arms are outstretched ahead with your palms facing down. As you lie in this position, consider the renewal of the scarab beetle that has been happening for millennia. Every year when the Nile River floods, the scarab beetle digs deep into the ground. When the waters recede, the beetle emerges renewed. As you lie in this position, dig deep into yourself by mentally scanning your entire body from the feet to the head. Do this three times over, observing how you feel along all the meridian points of your body. Once you have done this three times, focus on your solar plexus chakra. As you breathe in and out, consider how your diaphragmatic breathing is providing energy and oxygen to this chakra. See that energy growing as a yellow ball that expands to fill your whole body with yellow light. When you feel renewed, use your palms to push your body up and sit back on your haunches. Rest with your palms on the tops of your thighs for a few minutes. Now rise and stand to your feet so that you can engage in the comfort aspect of the meditation.

Stand with your feet shoulder-width apart. Lift your arms up at your sides so they are spread out level with your shoulders. Swing both arms backward while inhaling. Now bring your arms forward while exhaling. As you do this, imagine that Aset is standing behind you, mirroring your movements. When your hands reach the front of your body, allow one arm to cross your body below the other arm so that the hands do not touch each other. Instead, there should be a continual movement of your hands from the front of your body to the sides of your body as you breathe in and out. Repeat the movement and breathing exercise five times. Thereafter, bring your arms forward and cross them over each other in front of you in an embrace. Close your eyes and imagine Aset continuing to mirror your movements and holding you in an embrace. While in this position, breathe in and out five times. Say thank you to Aset, open your eyes, and step into the rest of your day.

KEMETIC PRAYER

Prayer is a conversation with God in a way that expects God to receive the message and respond to what is being put forth. Responses can be in the form of an audible voice, a vision, a dream, an event, or a series of coincidences that align with the response that you had sought in prayer.

Theurgical prayer is more than that. When practicing theurgy, we attempt to elevate our spirits to align closely with those of the gods and goddesses. When seeking solutions in the areas of our spiritual needs, we attempt to embody the personas of those gods and goddesses that have the knowledge and answers that we seek. It is in this way that we seek spiritual growth. The practice of theurgy is one whereby a close relationship with the deities is forged through the use of words, physical elements, and body movements that are associated with specific deities. This can be in the form of specific yoga movements, utterances of specific words or deity names, and rituals such as the lighting of candles or incense to bring about a spiritual atmosphere. This allows us to engage directly with and embody the deities through the combination of elements, actions, and words to create specific rituals for opening the pathway to alignment with them and enlightenment within ourselves.

Therefore, when practicing Kemetic Spirituality, the act of prayer goes beyond uttering a choice selection of words in a specific order. Although words do remain a part of the practice, Kemetic prayer requires greater input from you in that it requires you to be more in tune with the divine spirit that you wish to engage or embody. When you are in tune with or seek to be in tune with that divinity, you will use knowledge from your research to help you in your process. You will perform the actions, drink the drinks, and engage in the practices that you know that deity engaged in. You will also use visualization as a powerful means of bringing the words you are uttering to life. In this way, you will seek to embody them fully. One way of achieving this outcome is by using the methods and practices that you have been exposed to throughout this book.

Records of temple practices tell of the burning of incense over a fire or coals that were kept alight for this purpose. With time, we have moved away from multiple temple attendances throughout the day and are increasingly spending our times of worship in our personal spaces. This has necessitated a replacement for the open fires and hot coals upon which incense was initially burnt. Candles and incense in the form of sticks and cones have been the replacement that we have found. This has enabled us to continue the tradition and honor the gods.

In ancient Kemet, incense was lit at dawn, noon, and sunset as a means of enabling prayers to be lifted up to the heavens and attended to by the gods due to the sweet aroma that accompanied these prayers. The types of incense that were used differed based on the time of day. At dawn, frankincense was used. Midday was the time for myrrh, while dusk was the opportunity to light Kyphi. Kyphi was a complex incense. It was edible and used to cure illness while also burnt as an offering. Its composition involved multiple ingredients, such as honey, frankincense, mint, raisins, pine resin, pine kernels, cinnamon, myrrh, and juniper berries. Burning scented candles and incense at sunset has the additional benefit of making your dreams more vivid.

In addition to the daily incense, specific types of incense were used to call upon identified deities. For example, myrrh was used to invoke Asar, Auset, Hathor, and

Anubis. Anubis was additionally attracted by cedarwood and frankincense. Frankincense was also used to invoke Hathor. Using this knowledge, incense and scented candles for these specific deities may be burned at sunrise, midday, and sunset. Burning incense or scented candles is a good accompaniment for your prayers as you can follow the habits of the ancient Egyptians. Not having the opportunity to attend temple three times a day, you may choose to use scented smoke from fire in the form of incense and candles when you engage in prayer. This can attract the attention of the gods for attending to your requests.

In asking with the expectation of receiving, it is recommended that you practice gratitude like Hathor by holding a deep-seated belief that your prayers have already been answered. Practicing gratitude in this way enables you to maintain a state of Ma'at. It is also a good idea to declare events with the authority of Heru when he was in the form of Nefertum as he spoke creation into existence. By declaring something into existence, you go beyond asking and step into a belief that your requests will be fulfilled even as you ask them. When you do this, you will begin to use the universal energy that is described in the Hermetic laws and thus step into alignment with the power of the energy that you are embodying and invoking.

As you engage the right attitude and words, attempt to align your movements with the gods and goddesses. This is best done through the practice of Kemetic yoga, as depicted on the temple walls and papyrus scrolls. The Kemetic yoga bonus chapter that is included at the end of this book can provide you with some guidance on how to use yoga to embody the gods and goddesses. It will also provide you guidance on the movements you can use in tandem with some of the specific prayers provided later in this chapter. As your body aligns with divine actions, so too should your state of mind be in alignment with the divine. It is only with this state of mind that you can participate in the continual act of creation that is constantly occurring as the universe continues to expand outwards. By ensuring balance and harmony in your own life, you enable the same to occur in the universe. This is in accordance with the Hermetic law of correspondence that states, "As above, so below." When you do this, you become a co-creator of more than your life but of the universe as well. This is the state that is beneficial to aim toward living in on a daily basis.

Thus, it would be favorable if an all-encompassing prayer activity were a part of your daily life. Start each day with a prayer. If possible, do this between 4 a.m. and 6 a.m., which is the start of the day. It allows you to align your intentions with the sun itself just before it makes its daily journey across the sky.

This time of the day is quietest in terms of lack of disturbance from the day's activities and from the electronic devices that interfere with our focus as they compete for our attention. You will be in a quieter state of mind than the rest of the day. The early part of the day after waking up is also the time when your conscious and subconscious minds are more connected to each other, having just emerged from the dream world. Refrain from turning to technology first thing in the morning as it vibrates at a different frequency to your body and soul. Additionally, the minute you turn on the television, radio, or mobile phone, your attention will be redirected. You will no longer be focused internally on yourself and your spirit guides as you should be. Instead, your attention will be hijacked by time-consuming technology and media. If you want to grow spiritually, this is an integral time of the day for spiritual connection and reflecting on any messages that you may have received from the divine in the form of dreams.

If you remember your dreams, take time to play through them as you try to recall them in detail. Ask for guidance in understanding any messages that may have come through from your spirit guides in dream format. It is a good idea to keep a dream journal in which you can record any dreams that you remember. This will allow you to track any recurring themes to help determine if there is a special message being communicated to you. If your dreams are prophetic, giving a warning or announcement of a future event, having a written record will provide you with evidence that the prophecy came before the actual occurrence. This will strengthen your belief in the messages you receive and help you pick up on any patterns that can be applied to interpreting dreams in the future. If you have an understanding of the dream, ask for divine assistance in knowing what steps to take to implement any actions that may have been suggested by the dream or to know what steps to take next to manifest your desires. If you have no understanding of the dream, look for themes, people, places, and events that contain meaning for your subconscious mind. This can provide guidance in mapping the symbols and archetypes from your dreams to those in the world around you.

When you perform your daily prayers, always do so with a spirit of gratitude and with the intention of living your life in balance with the laws of the universe. In your prayers, reflect on the laws of Ma'at and ask for guidance in those areas that you feel you are weakest in your ability to uphold. Take time to mention the areas of necessity in your life and request provision in those areas. When invoking Ma'at, specific combinations of incense you can use include amber and myrrh; gardenia and rose; lavender and sage; frankincense and sandalwood; jasmine and vanilla; white sage and dragon's blood; patchouli and bergamot; and citrus and cedarwood. Any of these combinations can be lit before you start your prayer ritual.

Pray for the health of your body, in particular, the essential body organs referred to as the children of Heru. Ask for health for your liver, lungs, stomach, and intestines. Ask that they be protected by Imsety, Hapi, Duamutef, and Qubehsenuf, respectively. Ask that they do this with the assistance of Isis, Nephthys, Neith, and Selket in the same manner that these deities will protect these organs in the afterlife. Ask for clarity and guidance on how to take care of these organs to ensure a long and healthy life.

SPECIFIC PRAYERS

As you pray, be aware that different deities are in charge of different areas of life. Therefore, you should try to direct your prayers according to your prevalent needs at any given time. A targeted prayer is more likely to result in the specific outcome that you need than you would experience by praying a blanket prayer. Although these blanket prayers cover all areas, they also draw attention to those areas that do not require immediate attention. Because they are such generic prayers, you may not register the results when they do occur. Remember that when you pray, not only are you invoking the gods and goddesses, but you are also engaging with the universal forces. Therefore, a focused attitude is necessary to enable you to have the strongest impact possible. To achieve such focus, it is advisable to start with some meditation first. This will clear your mind of unnecessary thoughts, enabling you to bring only your request into the conversation with the deities, leaving any negativity and frustrations behind you.

The following are a few targeted prayers to guide you on how you can format your prayers to achieve specific outcomes. In each of the prayers below, the deities that are invoked are those that preside over the areas in which they are called upon for assistance. The prayers end in gratitude, for you need to have the belief that your prayers will be answered; in this way, you will manifest your words. You can enhance these prayers by using the corresponding yoga movements containing the names of the deities if these are listed in the Kemetic Yoga chapter. This will help you focus your attention and embody the deity that you are invoking for assistance.

FOR FARMERS and Gardeners

This morning as I go out to plant my seed, I reach out to Geb, god of the earth. Let the soil that I plant my seed into be rich and fertile, with the perfect mineral combination for my needs. I also open the works of my hand to Ausar, god of fertile vegetation. I ask you to be favorable to me. Guide my hand in my planting and my harvesting, even as you guide my plants in the growing process. I ask that my garden might honor you and the work that you did while on earth. I ask that you protect my plants from pests, droughts, and heavy weather. In this request, I also call upon Tefnut, who is goddess of moisture in the air. Let there be the right amount and the right kind of precipitation at the right time. I ask that this precipitation will help my plants to flourish to the best of their capacity. Help me to make a positive impact in my community through my harvest. By the power of Amen-Ra. Thank you.

FOR LEGAL MATTERS

As I embark on the activities that relate to this legal matter (name the specific activities and the legal matter), I ask for intervention from Ma'at and Djehuti. You two who maintain truth, wisdom, and honor in the world, I ask that you maintain these aspects within my life. I ask that the wisdom of Djehuti should be present in the minds of those who will be presiding over my matter. I ask that this same wisdom should be present during the preparation phase for the due date. Wisdom of Djehuti, I invite you to sit alongside my legal representatives. Let them be inspired with the right approach to tending to the matter before us. Let me also be inspired with a good memory to remember important details in time, details that can fruitfully contribute to the preparation process. I ask that Sekhmet be present to protect me in my innocence and ensure that the outcome of this legal matter is one that is fair to me. I ask that Ma'at be ever-present to ensure that justice prevails in this matter and in all related activities. By the power of Amen-Ra. Thank you.

FOR HEALING From Physical Disease

Bastet, I invoke you now in my time of need. I ask for your intervention as I battle with this disease that has consumed me and reduced the richness of my life to a fraction of what I once enjoyed. I ask you, oh protector of households, to protect me and my household in this time of need. Come into my life, into my household, and dwell within it, driving away any evil spirits that may be the cause of this illness. Please bring health back into my body and vitality into my life. Please restore my household back to its former glory and make it even greater than we can imagine. Restore my body to the good conduit of spirit that it is meant to be. Let your goodness and mercy dwell within me and my household. By the power of Amen-Ra. Thank you.

FOR SUCCESSFUL MEDICAL Operations

Heru-Ur, god of health and restoration. I ask that you restore my body to its full functionality. Even as I go into the operation room today, I ask that you guide the doctors in their duties so that I may be fully restored. I ask you, Nephthys, to look after my internal organs during this procedure. Let the doctors' hands be sure and steady so that they only operate on the intended organ and no mistakes are made to either side of the intended operation area. I also call upon Iusaaset, goddess of life, that my body may be fully healed after the successful procedure. I ask you, Aset, with your power to resurrect, that you cover me with your resurrection power. Let all anesthetic procedures proceed without glitches, allowing me to sleep and wake up from the operation at the correct time. Thank you for resurrecting me from the anesthesia. I thank you now for doing this when the time is right for me to wake up, and not before. I present this prayer by the power of Amen-Ra. Thank you.

FOR TRAVEL and Foreign Relations

Oh, Het-Heru, goddess over diplomacy and foreign nations. We ask that you be with us now. Guide us on our journey and in all our interactions, both planned and unplanned. We pray for all travel plans to go smoothly, both in relation to transportation and with regard to any documentation that is needed. Let all our negotiations during the route to and from our destination, as well as at our destination, be favorable toward us. Let the people of the foreign land (here you can say the name of the country) that we are about to enter view us as welcome allies. Let us have good and fruitful relations with them. May these be relationships that will last many happy years and that are beneficial to all sides. We call upon Anpu that we may not get lost on our journey but that we may be free to explore and find our way back home safely. We call upon Set to govern the events of our journey. May everything go peacefully and according to plan. Please keep chaos at bay. Let the weather also be favorable for the purposes of our journey, that there be no interference from nature in a way that can impede our progress as we go about our journey. Thank you to you, Anpu, Set, and Het-Heru, for guiding us on this journey and in all the interactions that we will have surrounding it. By the power of Amen-Ra. We thank you.

FERTILITY FOR MEN

Oh, Ausar and Auset, please help me now during my time of need. Aset, you brought life to a dead phallus. Please bring life into this phallus of mine so that it may be productive. Ausar, you fathered Heru even though you were no longer in this world, and your phallus had been swallowed by a crocodile. Please imbue me with the capability that you had when you mated with Auset in such a way as to be productive even in your spiritual form. Please resurrect in me the ability to father children in this lifetime. I thank you, Ausar and Auset, for inspiring me at this moment with the example of your ability to reproduce even when it seemed that hope was lost. Thank you for restoring hope in me today. Please make me resolute and guide my actions so that I, too, can be the proud father to healthy offspring. By the power of Amun-Ra. Thank you.

FERTILITY FOR WOMEN

Oh, Hathor, beautiful mother and protector of women, I ask you to protect my womb and associated organs today. I ask for your assistance in the conception process that I am undergoing. I ask that you guide me and bring joy into my life by making this conception fruitful. I know that I will use this successful event to embody the gratitude that you bring into the world. Thank you for loving women, for protecting them, and for providing them with so much beauty and joy. I ask now that my joy might be multiplied as I conceive the offspring that I so crave. I call upon you, Aset, to guide me in this process so that I might also nurse offspring in the same way that you nursed Heru. I thank you for being with me and for your guidance through this process. By the power of Amen-Ra. Thank you.

FOR A SUCCESSFUL CELEBRATORY Event

Hathor, you who brings pleasure, love, fun, and music

into our lives. We ask that you join us in celebration today. Thank you that we have an occasion to celebrate. May it be a joyful occasion for everybody who is in attendance. Bless each of them with a sense of gratitude, a soul filled with laughter, and a desire to have fun. Let there be a deep appreciation for everybody at the event, and let everybody feel fully included in the activities surrounding this celebration. I ask Bastet to provide us with good music that makes it additionally fun for everybody involved. Let that music become the backtrack to amazing memories for everyone in attendance. Let Ma'at be present at the event to ensure harmony among everyone and order in the proceedings. By the power of Amen-Ra, we thank you for a wonderful event.

For Exams, Thesis, and Other Writing

I call upon Djehuti today. You, who is god over the written word. I ask now, Djehuti, that you chase away the chaos from my mind as you daily chase away the chaos from Ra's boat as he traverses the Duat every night. Help me to do the work before me with a clear and organized mind, one that has no disturbance from any demons of doubt and forgetfulness. Let my writing be a clear and full expression of my well-thought-out ideas, providing insight to the readers of my words. Let there be no doubt about my level of intellect in the reading of the words that I write; instead, let those who encounter these words be enlightened and inspired in new ways. I pray also for the wisdom of Nehmetawy. I am in need today, and I ask for your support as protector of those in need. Please impart your wisdom to me and enable me to share the impact of that enhanced wisdom with those who will read my works. I thank you for your help, and I receive the goodness that you provide me with today. By the power of Amen-Ra. Thank you.

KEMETIC MORNING, MIDDAY, AND EVENING RITUALS

It is advantageous to do your best to start your morning with an attitude of gratitude. Have a sense of purpose for the day by maintaining your focus with some yoga and the right words directed at the sovereign deity for your day's purposes. A few examples are now given to guide you in creating your own morning rituals. These rituals include yoga poses, breathing exercises, and some words of prayer to help you become fully engaged in focusing on the deity and the purpose of the ritual.

BREATHING LIFE INTO THE DAY

Take time to sit still and in silence. Breathe in for a count of four. One, two, three, four. Remember to breathe deeply into your diaphragm so that your belly is extended by your inhalation. Now breathe out for a count of four: one, two, three, four. Stand up and stretch your arms way up above your head. Simultaneously, lift your heels so that you are standing on your tiptoes. While your arms are raised above your head, breathe in and out to the count of four. This is the Shu position, which fills your lungs with oxygen to energize you for the day.

Lower your arms so that they hang by your sides, and lower your heels so that your feet stand flat on the ground. Breathe in to the count of four before breathing out to the count of four. Consider the day before you in relation to the invigorating breath that you just took. What areas of your life do you want to breathe life into today? In this relaxed position, think of three or four areas that are most important to breathe life into today. Now raise your arms above your head again while lifting up your heels so that you stand on your toes. As you raise your arms, imagine that you are lifting up the first issue that needs life to be breathed into it for the day. As you are raising the issue up above your head, say out loud or in your mind, "Shu, I raise this matter up to you today. As I do so, I declare that I am letting go of any anxiety that I may have toward its successful resolution or completion. I declare that as I raise this matter up to you, it is no longer my concern alone, but it is also your concern. I thank you for carrying the bulk load of this issue. I ask that you breathe life into it."

When your arms are fully above your head, fold your hands back on your wrist as far as they will go. Your posture should be as though you were offering something up on a tray to somebody much taller than you. This is to fully hand the matter over to Shu to breathe life into it and remove any major concerns from yourself. Now breathe in to the count of four and then breathe out to the count of four before lowering your arms back to your sides and your feet back to the ground. Once you are back in a relaxed position, breathe in and out to the count of four again before raising up your next concern to Shu.

MIDDAY RECHARGE

If you have a demanding schedule, you will often find that by mid-afternoon, you run out of the energy needed to focus your attention on the work at hand. In such situations, it is important to take a break and reboot yourself in a manner that will enable you to work so that optimal output is provided. In such circumstances, take a short break to do a breathing exercise that will help you maximize your productivity once more.

If you are in an environment that allows you to do so, get into the lotus pose. To do this, sit cross-legged with your back straight and your palms facing upward. Taking time to do this reminds you that it is possible to be detached from the distractions around you while at the same time remaining focused on your intentions for the day. If your environment does not allow you to get into the lotus positions, find a chair where you can comfortably sit upright. Sit with your back straight and your palms facing upward.

Let the airflow into your lungs by inhaling through your nostrils. As your lungs fill, do not take a break between breaths, but immediately force the air out of your lungs and out your mouth. Contract your abdominal muscles to assist you with the process. As you sit in this position, continue to breathe in and out evenly in this manner. Whereas other exercises may require you to breathe in and hold your breath before exhaling, this requires you to breathe in and then immediately breathe out. Your inhalations and exhalations should be for the same length of time. For example, you could inhale for one second and exhale for one second. For a length of time that is between two to ten minutes, continue to inhale and exhale continually with no breaks between breaths.

As you do your breathing exercise, keep your mind focused on your positive intentions for the day and how you are going to bring the laws of Ma'at into the rest of the day's activities.

This type of breathing technique is called *Breath of Fire*. It invigorates you and will even help ease digestive problems if you have any. If you have challenges with your lungs, heart, or spine, you should avoid using this breathing technique, as rapid breathing puts pressure on those areas. As an alternative to using the breath of fire, use the box breathing technique. Box breathing requires you to breathe in for a count of four, hold your breath for a count of four, breathe out for a count of four, and again hold your breath for a count of four. Meditate on the laws of Ma'at. While box breathing may not invigorate you in the way that *Breath of Fire* will, you will be able to focus your mind better than before the energy slump occurred. You can then use this newfound focus to achieve the results you desire for the day.

EVENING RITUAL

End your day well so that your soul has a safe passage through the world of dreams every night. You may want to clear your mental state of any matters that arose during the day that distracted or disturbed you from your purpose. Find a quiet place to lie on your back and reflect on your day. While in this mummy pose with your arms relaxed at your sides, weigh the events of your day against the laws of Ma'at. While murder, violent robbery, and disrespecting the deceased are easy to avoid for most people, what about those laws that you have an opportunity to break daily? Some of these are laws relating to placing yourself on a pedestal (law 37); speaking angrily or arrogantly (law 35); wishing somebody ill (law 36); meddling in somebody else's business (law 30); embellishing the truth (law 31); eavesdropping (law 18); and lying (law 8). These are just some of the laws of Ma'at that will aid you if you are conscientious enough to uphold them.

Examine the responses you had to each situation that presented itself to you during the course of the day. This will help you identify those areas where you were unable to align your daily actions with your intention to live in Ma'at. Once you have identified these moments, do not judge yourself harshly. Instead, know that even if you have not succeeded in living in Ma'at on this day, your soul will guide you to overcome future hurdles. Be grateful that you have the capacity to identify these areas and reflect on solutions and responses that could have served the moment better. Forgive yourself for not having taken those actions, knowing that at the time the opportunity presented itself, you were not aware of the options immediately available to you. Be grateful for the wisdom you have gained during this moment of reflection. Experiential wisdom provides knowledge you can apply at a later stage in your life should similar situations arise again. Be grateful that your soul guides you through the challenging aspects of your life.

As you consider how your soul guides you through life, move from the resting mummy pose into the fish pose. Do this by sliding your upward-facing palms under your thighs. Then raise your torso off the ground while your body is supported by your elbows pressing into the ground. While in this position, breathe in deeply and exhale. You will find this easy to do as the position extends your chest capacity. Continue to breathe in and out slowly until you have done so five times. Now gently lower your body back to the ground. Resume the mummy position, moving your arms to the sides of your body. Breathe in and then breathe out again. As you do so, thank the Ntrs for their support of your activities throughout the course of the day. If you cannot think about things to be thankful for, consider the fact that you are alive and able to breathe. Consider the fact that you are on a spiritual journey that is moving you daily toward a state of enlightenment. Be grateful for this. Once you have exhausted the moment of meditating on your day, you may gently sit up. You may now enter into the remainder of your evening with a fresh outlook.

БЕКНМЕТ

✿ 9 ✿
BONUS KEMETIC YOGA FOR ENERGIZING YOUR MODERN DAY PRACTICE

S mai Tawi, or Kemetic Yoga, is a discipline that is inspired by the Kemetic creation story as well as by the postures of the Kemetic gods (Ntr) that are depicted on temple walls and papyruses. Despite the fact that the postures that inspire it have been available for humanity to see for thousands of years, it is only recently that the practice has been reconstructed into a series of yoga poses. By practicing these poses, you can strengthen your core muscles and improve your flexibility. The poses by themselves are a way to maintain a healthy body. However, as with all Kemetic practice, engaging in Smai Tawi involves more than just the activity of bending, stretching, and twisting your body. It is used in conjunction with other lifestyle activities to improve your overall health. This includes spiritual well-being coupled with additional activities such as drinking a lot of water and moving toward a plant-based diet that encourages a healthy body. The use of these poses, coupled with breath work, allows you to focus your energy toward maintaining the inner balance that is an essential part of the spiritual journey.

When you combine the poses with daily exposure to the sun, between 10 and 20 minutes, you create the optimal conditions for your body to thrive. The sun energizes your body, and daily exposure to its rays enables your body to produce disease-combating Vitamin D. The sun—Ra, the breath—Shu, and the yoga poses inspired by the different gods and goddesses will put your body in alignment with its natural composure. This state of body enables you to have the correct state of mind to deal with life's daily challenges. The process of Kemetic yoga requires you to meditate on the creation story and on the gods and goddesses with each pose and each transition to the next one. The addition of this meditative attitude is what makes Kemetic yoga the ideal practice for maintaining a healthy body, mind, and soul.

SHTI—THE MUMMY

The Mummy pose is a base position for many other poses. This is apt because this pose is both the beginning and the end position for a few other poses, reflecting its position as the beginning and end of life itself. As the beginning, it embodies potential. We never know what a new life will unfold into; therefore, there is excitement in witnessing this stage. It is a stage where there are multiple possibilities, as the choices that limit and focus our directional growth have not been made yet. Performed at the end, the Shti pose depicts a body that has been prepared for resurrection. This pose is taken at the end of a life that has been fully lived. All the potential has been expressed through various decisions that were made and actions that were taken. Looking at a body that has been prepared for resurrection, you know that there are few surprises that it can present you with. The pose is a symbol of Asar being resurrected by Aset. In resurrecting Asar, Aset overcomes the jealousy and ignorance of Set as she uses wisdom to bring Asar to life. When we look at the bodies of men and women of our time at the moment when their life is spent, we believe and hope that they will be resurrected into the afterlife. They have spent their potential on earth, and there is a new and different level of potential waiting for them in the afterlife. Therefore, their ending becomes similar to their beginning. They will have ended a chapter of all that is known to them, yet they are a step away from a new chapter, from starting at the beginning and the unknown with new possibilities once more.

Lie on your back with your feet shoulder-width apart. Consider the energy of the universe, which Aset used to bring Asar to life. Imagine this being directed toward you with love and compassion. Breathe in and out as you feel this universal energy embracing you as you become one with it. While you lie there, direct the universal energy toward any part of your body that needs healing.

THE LOTUS

The mummy pose flows into the Lotus Pose. These two poses combine to symbolize the move from death to life, which is the beginning of creation. The Lotus Pose is inspired by the beautiful lotus flower. The lotus is often found in muddy waters, yet it sits upright and detached. It continues to exude its beauty despite its surroundings. When we perform this pose, it is a reminder to remain detached from the distractions of the world around us and that we must remain steadfast to our true purpose of alignment with the divine through meditation and the study of spiritual practices.

Doing this movement requires you to begin by imagining the world before creation. You can then rise from the dead waters of chaos into the stillness of the lotus flower. Therefore, start by lying on your back with your arms relaxed at your sides. Lay perfectly still with your eyes closed. Breathe in and out while thinking of all the potential that you have within you to create. The potential within you is the ability to make something beautiful from the chaos that existed before creation. Lie in this position for two minutes before sitting up in the lotus position.

For the lotus position, sit cross-legged on your yoga mat with each foot tucked under the calf of the opposite leg. Keep your back straight and rest your forearms on your knees with your palms facing upwards.

If you are very flexible, you may cross your legs in such a way that your feet rest on top of your thighs.

Should you have difficulty sitting cross-legged, sit up straight with your knees tucked underneath your body, allowing your back to align with your heels. Rest your wrists on your thighs so that your palms can face upwards.

In this position, your body is centered, and the chakras (or energy centers) along your spinal column are aligned.

Both positions of this movement are good for meditation and reflection while engaged in breathing exercises.

When doing your breathing exercises, avoid quick, shallow breaths that lift the shoulders and expand the chest. These movements should only happen if the breathing exercises specifically incorporate these actions. You should instead practice diaphragmatic breathing. This is done by inhaling through your nose in such a way as to allow your stomach to expand. Hold the breath in your abdomen for two seconds, and then exhale through your mouth.

NEFERTEM ON THE LOTUS

This pose is inspired by Heru, The Divine Child of Creation when he is in the form of Nefertum or Nefertem. During the creation process, Heru sits on a lotus flower while divine consciousness is creating the universe through the use of sound vibration.

To engage in this pose, start in the lotus position. Thereafter, lift your index finger to point to your mouth, from which sound emanates. Return your hand to your lap and recite the names of the gods and goddesses in accordance with the order they ascend in on the tree of life: Heru Ur, Nebthet, Set, Aset, Asar, Nut, Tefnut, Geb, Shu, Hetheru, Ma'at, Ra. During the process, take time to look around the room. Focus on each object in the room. Remind yourself that each physical object you lay eyes on has been created from primeval matter. Now close your eyes and imagine that you have assumed the qualities of Heru in his child form as Nefertem. Imagine that, as you were naming the gods and goddesses from the creation story, they were being created so that they could take their place in the universe. In this form of Nefertem, sitting on top of the lotus flower, unbothered by the chaos around you, begin to imagine yourself creating your universe according to your desires. Now, having created your ideal universe, see yourself detached from it, like a pristine lotus flower in the middle of a swampy lake. Your perfection is unaffected by your surroundings. Even if the world around you is in chaos, you continue to embody the qualities that you were born to express.

NUN

This pose is inspired by the act of Ra emerging from the waters of Nun during the creation process.

As Ra is a god that is in balance and unifies opposites, start this pose in a similarly balanced squatting position. Keep your feet parallel to each other and your palms pressed against each other in front of your chest. Breathe in as you imagine yourself in total alignment beneath the waters of Nun. Exhale. Breathe in and out again, knowing that you have the potential of creation within you. This potential for creation is the same energy potential that was used to create the universe.

Calm your mind from any chaotic thoughts that may appear, and rise. As you rise, your first motion will be from a squatting to a semi-squatting position. While you are rising, begin to inhale and move your arms apart in an upward movement so that your palms are on either side of your head. Your elbows must be bent so that your upper arms are parallel to the floor while your forearms are parallel to each other on either side of your head.

Exhale while bending your wrists backward slightly so that your palms appear to be pushing up against the sky. At this point, complete the pose by engaging the second motion. This requires you to continue rising into a fully standing position.

WARM-UP

This warm-up pose is a preparation for the separation of heaven (Nut) from the earth (Geb).

- Start your warm-up by standing with your feet shoulder-width apart and with your arms stretched out. Twist your upper body such that with each twist, you are looking behind you. Inhale as you turn toward the right, and exhale as you turn toward the left. With each turn of your body, feel the air flowing around your hands and your arms.
- Now place your hands on your waist and bend sideways to your left side. Feel the stretch along the right side of your torso. Now bend to the other side to balance the effect on your body.
- Now bend backward slightly before bending forward at your waist while your hands are still on your waist. Do this four times for each direction.
- Next, lean forward from the waist and then start tilting toward the left before tilting backward, then to the right, and forward again. This moves your body in a clockwise circular motion. When you have made the movement three times, repeat the activity, but this time circle in the opposite direction. Then bend forward and tilt your body to the right.

Continue to do this until you have moved your torso in a circular form.

- Bring your palms together in front of your chest in the Hetep posture that emulates a praying position. Inhale deeply, imagining that you are inhaling peace. Now exhale deeply. Imagine that you are exhaling all the tension out and away from your body. Repeat the process three times, making sure that you maintain diaphragmatic breathing throughout the process.

- Now drop your hands down to your sides in preparation for some neck stretching movements. To begin stretching your neck, drop your head forward so that you can feel the muscles stretching out at the back of your neck. Now look upward to drop your head back in a way that will stretch the throat area. Then incline your head toward the left ear so that the right side of your neck is stretched. Thereafter incline your head toward the right ear so that the left side of the neck is stretched. Do this four times in each direction to ensure that your neck is adequately stretched on the front, back, left, and right.

- Circle your head to the left four times, then circle your head to the right four times.

SHU

Shu created heaven—Nut—and earth—Geb—and is the space between them in the form of air or ether. When combined with moisture—Tefnut—air becomes the life-sustaining force energy known as Sekhem.

This yoga position, therefore, emphasizes the breath and the space between earth and heaven, in the same way that the god Shu separated the initial connection between Geb and Nut.

From a relaxed standing position, raise your arms above your head. During the process, breathe in deeply and raise up to stand on your tiptoes. Now exhale while lowering your heels so that you are no longer standing on your tip toes but are back to standing with your feet flat on the floor. At the same time, lower your arms back to your sides. Say the name of Shu during the exhalation process to match the air that you are breathing out. Visualize yourself as being at one with the universe and as the creator of your existence.

JOURNEY OF RA

Atem Ra—also known as Tem or Atum—is the setting sun. This represents the moment when Nut, the god of the heavens, engages in the daily consumption of Ra. Once consumed, Ra needs to travel through the Duat—the underworld. Here, he battles with the entities of the underworld until he becomes Ra Khepri, the rising sun, where Nut gives birth to him in the east.

Ra's daily journey into the underworld inspires a series of poses that demonstrate how the process of creation is a continuous activity that permeates through all aspects of our lives. There are six postures indicated. They need to be performed in succession to complete the full series. Once they have been completed, they are then repeated in the reverse mode to create a total of 12 postures. The fact that the series consists of 12 postures is symbolic of the 12 gates that Ra needs to travel through during his daily journey through the Duat (The underworld. The place Ra goes to between sunset and sunrise.)

Your mental attitude during the performance of this series is recommended to be one of peace, self-service, and consistency. These attributes are a reflection of Ra as he battles through the underworld every night to provide his life-giving force to creation on a daily basis.

- Start off the series in a standing position. Put your hands in front of you with palms pressed together in a prayer mode while you exhale.

- Raise your arms up in front of you and then over your head while inhaling. Now, arching your upper back, bend your torso backward, and reach up with your hands toward Ra —the sun.

- Now exhale as you bend forward, bringing the sun with you, hastening it toward the sunset as you lean forwards. In bending forward, keep your back straight, and your arms stretched forward on either side of your neck.
- Continue bending forward until you are folded over, with your hands on either side of your ankles. If you are flexible enough to do so, put your hands flat on the floor on either side of you

to symbolize Ra going deep into the
underworld.

- While inhaling, stretch out your right leg
  behind you, lowering your body as you do so.
  Use your palms or fingertips to keep yourself
  steady on the ground as you extend your torso
  upwards and look toward the sky.

- Now tuck your head back down so that your
  face is toward the ground. While holding your
  breath, push your left leg out so that it is parallel
  to your right leg. Keep your head down between
  your arms while your heels lie flat on the floor,

providing a good stretch to both your upper and lower body. Your body will form an inverted V, which is the Nut pose. This point in the series symbolizes the point at which the goddess Nut consumes the sun, Ra, before his journey into the Duat underworld.

- Exhale as you lower yourself to the floor, knees first. Arch your lower back while lowering your chest to the floor. Put your hands palm-down on either side of your chest to support your body. If you feel comfortable enough, you may also lower your forehead to the floor in addition to your chest. This signifies the beginning of the journey into the underworld.

- Bring your waist and pelvis down to the floor while inhaling. At the same time, push down on the floor with your palms while arching your back and keeping your elbows bent and close to your body. This is the cobra pose. While performing the cobra pose, you should keep your focus on the point between your eyebrows, the third eye, which is the sixth energy center. At this time, you are halfway through the journey of Ra.

- To begin the second half of the journey, lift the middle of your body back into the inverted V. Once in this Nut pose, exhale with your heels and forehead pressed toward the floor.

- Next, bring your right foot forward so that it lies between your hands. At the same time, inhale, bending back your neck so that your face looks toward the sky. Push down toward the ground with your pelvis to enable you to stretch well.

- Bring your left foot forward to join your right foot. Exhale as you do so, allowing your head to hang and your body to bend over. Your arms and neck should be almost parallel, and your palms must be as flat on the floor as you are able to make them.

- Stand up and raise your hands above your head, inhaling as you do. Reach your hands above your head and back. In this position, you will symbolically put Ra up into the sky, where he will assume his position as the rising sun—Ra Khepri.

- Exhale as you bring your arms down and into a prayerful position. Drop your arms to your sides. You have completed one cycle of the journey.

Repeat the entire journey with a focus on your left leg instead of your right one. You can go through the process about six to eight times. The best time to do this sequence is first thing in the morning. When you have completed the number of repetitions you would like to make, assume the mummy pose.

SHOULDER STAND

This is also known as the Geb shoulder stand. Geb is the earth. When earth separates from heaven, or when Geb separates from Nut, there are several exercises that he performs. The shoulder stand and the plough exercise that follow it are exercises that flow into each other. They are among other earth exercises performed by Geb.

Begin this exercise by lying on your back with your arms at your sides. Lift your legs straight up while keeping them parallel to each other. Use your hands to support your back at the waist, allowing your shoulders to support the weight of your body.

This pose is good for the entire body. However, using it will especially help you gain extra strength in your back, spine, and neck areas. It will also benefit the upper energy centers of the spiritual body.

PLOUGH

From the shoulder stand, gently bring your legs over your head so that your toes touch the floor above your head. If you are not flexible enough to touch the floor with your toes, do not force it. Extend your legs as far as they will go beyond your head. You will develop more flexibility over time.

Return your arms to the sides of your body and hold the position for five seconds. Unfurl your legs until you are lying flat on your back again.

WHEEL

The wheel pose strengthens the back, arms, and legs.

Lie on your back with your knees bent and the soles of your feet flat against the ground and close to your buttocks. Lift up your arms above your head. Place your hands on the ground above your head, with your fingers pointing toward the toes and your palms flat against the ground. Inhale as you lift your body up off the ground by pushing against the ground using your hands and feet. Hold the position for as long as you are able. Exhale as you slowly bring your torso down to the ground. As you lie on the ground, breathe in and out deeply, meditating on Geb and Nut together at the time before the separation of heaven and earth.

FISH

This pose is best done after the shoulder and plough poses. This will help to balance the effect on your body.

To start off this pose, lie on your back with your arms at your side in the mummy pose. Put your hands next to your thighs with the palms facing up. Now slide your hands just under the edge of your thighs and lift your upper body up so that you rest on your elbows. Lift up your torso so that it is inverted, with your chest sticking out and your head extended backward to touch the floor.

In this position, with your head, elbows, and buttocks touching the floor while your chest is extended, your lungs can expand to their full capacity. Therefore, from this position of extended chest capacity, take five deep abdominal breaths. Inhale and exhale slowly while ensuring that you keep your lower body at ease.

Doing the fish pose reminds us of the two fish that accompanied Ra's boat as he sailed on the waters of Nun during the process of creation. As you breathe, consider your higher self and how it leads you on your spiritual journey toward enlightenment.

Once finished with the breathing exercise, bring your head forward to your chest and lower yourself down on your elbows so that you return to the mummy position. Once in the mummy pose, breathe deeply into your abdomen and exhale.

FORWARD BEND

From the mummy position, sit up straight with your feet stretched out in front of you. Ensure that you are positioned in such a way that you are sitting on your pelvic bone. Flex your feet in such a way that your toes point back toward your torso.

Do this three times: lift your arms above your head as you breathe in, then bring your arms down as you exhale. Each time you bring your arms down, reach forward to touch your toes while keeping your back straight. As you bend over, think about Nut, who bends over the earth and encloses the atmosphere; Shu and Tefnut create the life force within her body arch as she bends toward the earth (Geb).

Once you have completed the three repetitions, slowly lie down on your back and assume the mummy position.

The forward bend stretches the entire spinal column and massages internal organs such as the kidneys, the digestive system, and the liver.

SPINAL TWIST

The spine enables the body to function harmoniously by acting as a conduit between the brain and the rest of the body.

Start this exercise from a seated position with both legs extended in front of you. Bend the knee of your right leg while lifting up the right foot and placing it over and next to the left knee. Place your left hand on the floor behind you as you twist your body and look back over your left shoulder. Rest your right hand on your right knee. Walk your left hand back by moving it backward on the ground. As you do so, you will feel a stretch on the left side of your torso. Breathe in and out while in this position before walking your hand back to the body and twisting your body back to face forward with your legs stretched out in front of you. Now twist your spine in the other direction by lifting the foot of your left leg and placing it over the right leg. Put your left hand on your left knee. Meanwhile, support your body by placing your right hand on the floor. Lean your body back to stretch out the right side of your body as you walk your right hand backward. Once you have slowly inhaled and exhaled, return to the forward-facing position with your legs extended in front of you.

SELKET

Selket is the scorpion goddess. The scorpion has the power to protect by inflicting pain. In the creation story, Ra sent seven scorpions to protect the fleeing Aset while Set was trying to kill her.

To do the scorpion pose, start by lying on your belly with your forehead touching the ground. With fisted hands, stretch your arms out in front of you. Inhale as you lift up your left leg and exhale as you bring the left leg down. Repeat the process with the right leg. Now gently lift up both legs together, inhaling as you lift your legs up and exhaling as you bring your legs down.

You can repeat the exercise with your arms under your body rather than spread out in front of you.

This exercise is beneficial for the lower back.

SEBEK

Sebek is a crocodile god that represents the power of nature. Sebek is associated with the second energy center. Crocodiles were considered the most powerful animals in ancient Egypt. In the creation story, the crocodile assisted Asar.

Lie face-down on the ground with bent arms placed palm down on either side of your head. Bring your left knee up toward your left elbow. Straighten your left leg and then bring your right knee up toward your right elbow before straightening it. Repeat this exercise three to five times, alternating between both legs. Once you have finished the exercise, return to a sitting position and move your shoulders and back to shake out any tension that may be in those areas.

ARAT

Arat Sekhem is "serpent power." This is represented by Uraeus—the cobra. The cobra is connected with the resurrection of Asar in the creation story. Therefore, when you do the pose, consider the power of resurrection within your body. Also, be mindful of the Uraeus energy that rises from the tailbone to the forehead as spiritual awareness is reached. In Egyptian spirituality, this is the movement of Asar's energy along the djed tree as it grows out of the coffin in which he was trapped by his brother. In the yoga practiced in India, the rising Uraeus energy is referred to as the *kundalini*.

Lie on your stomach with your hands placed palm down below your shoulders and your forehead touching the ground. Inhale while raising your chest off the ground without using your hands to lift you off the ground. Exhale as you relax your body downwards so that your forehead touches the ground again. Rest for a moment before repeating the process. Do this three times before pushing your body up with your hands as high as you can, and hold the position for as long as it is comfortable for you to do so. Thereafter, relax your body back to ground level.

This exercise strengthens the thoracic area. It is associated with the spinal column and the development of the energy centers in your body. It also relates to a raising in consciousness and the psycho-spiritual energy levels of the body.

HOREMAKHET—THE SPHINX

The sphinx is related to the gods Set and Apuat and represents a human being who has reached enlightenment while retaining control of their lower spiritual self. In doing this pose, visualize your power to be as great as that of a lion, embracing the full alignment of your mind, body, and spirit. This is the power of the sphinx.

Take a kneeling position while resting on your heels. Now lean forward with your hands stretched out in front of you while using your elbows to support your body. Thereafter, straighten your elbows in order to raise your upper body. You should feel the strengthening effects on your back. Drop back down to your elbows and repeat the exercise.

HERU—HORUS

Heru balances the higher and lower self while defending truth, justice, and honor. He overcomes unrighteousness, death, and ignorance. In the creation story, he defeated the unenlightened Set—ignorance and injustice. He also helped resurrect his father, Asar.

Stand tall with your arms at the side of your body. In this position, see yourself as a strong, immovable pyramid. From this position of strength, imagine yourself as the maker of your destiny and the redeemer of your soul. Imagine yourself possessing all the qualities of Heru, such as a balance between the higher and lower self, while defending honor and justice.

HENU SERIES

This is a series of poses that pay homage to Apnu, Heru, and Set. The series is symbolic of joy and praise.

From a standing position, kneel with your right knee on the ground and the left knee pointing toward the sky.

Extend your upward-facing left hand away from your body. At the same time, hold your fisted right hand close to your chest.

Make a fist with your left hand and bring it to your chest. Then lift your right hand to the sky with your elbow bent at a right angle to the ground.

Return to a standing position and repeat the exercise using the alternate limbs.

NUT

Nut is the sky that encloses the ether and reaches to the earth's horizon.

To begin the exercise, stand with your arms raised above your head. Inhale. Now exhale as you lean over, slowly bending down until you can grasp your ankles. If you need to bend your knees to reach your ankles, then do so. Next, put your hands on the ground and walk them forward so that you create an inverted V shape with your body. Breathe in and out slowly before walking your hands back toward your ankles and then returning to a standing position with your arms held up above your head.

Visualize Nut in the form of the sky stretching over the earth as you do this exercise.

MA'AT

Ma'at is the goddess of balance who weighs each individual's soul to determine whether they are worthy enough to pass through to the afterlife.

Stand with your feet shoulder-width apart, and your arms stretched out on either side. Kneel in such a way that your left knee is touching the ground while your right knee is pointing upward with the right foot firmly on the ground. Twist your body toward the left. Turn your head to the right and twist your body so that your right arm is directly over your right knee. From this position, breathe in and out slowly while considering the areas in your life where you demonstrate a sense of balance.

Stand up and repeat the exercise for the other side of the body. This time, turn your head to the left and kneel with your left knee pointing to the sky. When you twist your body, do it so that your left arm is over your left knee.

While performing the exercise, think about how you will embody the principles of Ma'at within your life. These principles are truth, righteousness, and justice.

ASET WINGED—THE VICTORY POSE

Aset is the daughter of Nut and wife to Asar. She embodies spiritual and intellectual wisdom.

Stand with your feet together. Inhale as you extend your arms to either side. While exhaling, drop to your left knee. Keep your right foot flat on the ground so that your right knee is bent and pointing skyward. From a kneeling position, lower your body so that you are almost sitting on your left foot. Inhale and exhale while in this position. Then stand up and repeat the exercise with the left knee pointing upward.

ASET SITTING—THE THRONE POSE

Aset represents the physical body that supports the spiritual essence—Asar. In so doing, Aset is the throne that provides the spirit being with a physical way to manifest itself on earth.

Put your arms out in front of you with the palms facing downwards. Bend your knees and lower your body as though you were in the process of sitting down on a throne. Lower your body as far as it is comfortable for you to do so.

Visualize the goddess Aset supporting you in this pose. Inhale and exhale. Stand up and repeat the exercise.

AUSET EMBRACE

Hept, the Auset Embrace, is a pose that represents the goddess Auset in the process of embracing Ausar and Heru. This occurred after she brought Auset back to life and thus was able to conceive Heru. When you perform this pose, consider yourself resurrecting all the aspects of your life that you may have considered to be dead. This includes the psychological, physical, and spiritual aspects of your life. All your hopes and dreams can be brought to life with the administration of Auset's love.

Assume a standing position while you move your arms forwards and backward. Visualize yourself as Aset. Bring both arms forward to cross over in front of your chest in a loving embrace. Stand in this position while breathing in and out deeply.

DJED

The Djed pillar symbolizes the spinal column and the life force energy that it embodies. It is associated with the god Ptah. He cut down the Djed tree in order to enjoy its sweet aroma in his palace. It was only later that he found out that Asar was trapped within the tree.

Cross your arms over your chest, making fists with your hands. Envision yourself encased in a pillar the way Asar was. From this upright position, imagine yourself as a conduit between heaven and earth, united with divine consciousness.

The Djed represents spiritual enlightenment, steadfastness, and the Duat, or astral realm.

HEADSTAND

Kneel and bend forward. Clasp your hands one on top of the other so that your forearms form a V-shape with your elbows. Put your head down on the ground so that your hands support the top of your head. Straighten your legs so that your body moves upwards. Straighten your back and bring your legs up, bending them at the knee above your body as you find balance. Finally, extend your legs to a full standing position with your body fully supported by your hands.

If you have difficulty doing the headstand without support, do the exercise while facing a wall. This will enable you to use the wall as support to steady your body.

A variation of this exercise may be done with the hands placed on the ground, shoulder-width apart, and fingers splayed. Place your head on the ground in between them, using your hands for support as you lift yourself off the ground.

To come down from the headstand, bend your knees and then swing your legs forward as you extend them until your feet touch the ground.

KHEPRI—SCARAB BEETLE

Ra Khepri is the morning sun that emerges renewed every morning after going into the Duat as Ra Tem at the end of the previous day. Khepri is also the scarab beetle. The scarab beetle renews its body every year by burrowing into the mud when the Nile River floods. Once the waters recede, it emerges with a new body. Therefore, Khepri symbolizes the capacity for renewal.

To assume the Khepri pose, kneel while sitting back on your haunches. Extend your hands in front of you on the ground with the palms facing downward. Lean forward until your forehead touches the ground. Maintain this pose while reflecting on the renewal that is experienced by the scarab beetle every year. See this applied to your physical, mental, and spiritual well-being.

Kemetic yoga uses Sekhem (life force energy) in the

form of breath to help you focus universal energy within you. The meditation inspired by the various poses helps you ascend the tree of life. This occurs when you reflect on the parallels between the deities, the creation story, and your own life. Use these poses daily to assist you with your spiritual journey. Even if Kemetic yoga is the only practice that you start with, you will find that doing so fulfills multiple aspects of the requirements for the Kemetic lifestyle.

AFTERWORD

As we come to the end of the book, I wish you love and light on your spiritual journey. You have been equipped with the knowledge and insight to know which steps to take for each upcoming phase of your progression. As you continue on your journey, I pray that you maintain a spirit of peace, balance, and harmony. I hope that this book will be a constant companion with you on that journey as you turn to it often for guidance on the best steps to follow as you encounter different aspects of your life. Remember to carry a sense of Ma'at through all aspects of your life. If you are successful in this, know that it will end well with you. If you are having challenges with a sense of balance, find small things in life that you can be grateful for. Gratitude is the key to harmony because you receive more of what you are grateful for. As you express joy in the small events, you will find that greater reasons for being grateful will appear in your life. Use this principle of correspondence to ensure that you continually live in Ma'at.

As you live your life's purpose, remember that you will need courage for many things. You will encounter opposition and may even need to do battle with those that would harm your good intentions. As you encounter the Set personas in your journey, remember that you can call upon Asar, Heru, and Aset to guide and inspire you. In addition to this, you can call on other spirit guides in the form of your ancestors or even famous personalities that you have admired in the past. You are never truly alone in your daily battles. Remember this and ask for help accordingly.

What will help you tremendously is to maintain a clean diet in accordance with the requirements for a true initiate. A clean diet will turn your body into an effective vessel for your spirit. This makes it an essential building block of your spiritual walk. A healthy body that is not spending excess energy resources trying to digest inaccessible food will divert that energy to more spiritual pursuits. The building of your mental and spiritual life will benefit you.

Your prayers, yoga, and meditation will assist you further. They will provide you with the focus necessary to accomplish your goals in alignment with the universal laws evidenced in the Hermetic principles. Keep a pure heart and always look toward the goodness of the light.

One of the last things I would like to share with you is the knowledge that I am grateful for you. I am grateful for the need you had that allowed me the opportunity to write this book, for in the writing of it, I have also been inspired to embark on a journey. A journey that has required me to know more and to dig deeper so that I can share meaningful and practical information with you. This has required me to revisit, explore, experience, and prove the concepts mentioned in the book. As a result, I have come to a greater awareness of universal principles and the magic of Kemet, which has been hiding in plain sight all these years and in various forms. These forms have expressed themselves through the evolution of religion, lessons in wisdom, and nature itself. When we take time to observe nature, we realize that it is always in balance and its needs are provided for without constant striving. There is a rhythm to the inter-action between various aspects of nature. The more we observe this, the more we realize that every aspect of nature serves a purpose. As you align yourself with Ntr, may you also live in your purpose, finding mutually beneficial inter-actions along the way. Go now and enlighten others as you go along. I wish you well on your journey.

NUT and GEB

GLOSSARY

Ab: Heart Chakra, the energy center that governs the heart.

Abrahamic: Biblical. With Abraham as the central father figure.

Acacia: A flat-topped tree with rough bark with medicinal properties. It is native to Africa and Australia.

Altar: A place set aside as a meeting place between an individual or individuals and the divine. A place of worship.

Amen: Ra, the sun god.

Amen-Ra: Ra, the god of the sun.

Amun: Ra, the sun god.

Amun-Raa: The sun god, Ra.

Ancestors: Previous generations of your family tree.

Ankh: A cross with a loop above the horizontal bar instead of a continuation of the vertical shaft. Also known as the Egyptian cross, it represents life.

Anpu: Anubis, the protector of graves.

Anubis: Jackal-headed god of funerals and protector of graves.

Apep: Apophis, the snake that tries to consume Ra as he traverses the underworld.

Apollo: The name the Greeks gave to Heru-Ur or Horus.

Apophis: An evil snake that Ra needs to fight against every night as he journeys through the underworld.

Arat Sekhem: Serpent power.

Asar: Ausar, also know as Osiris.

Aset: Auset. She restored her husband to life after he was stuck in a pillar. She later collected his dismembered body for a dignified burial.

Astrology: Studying the correlation between the stars and a person's life events. This is especially done in relation to celestial alignment at one's time of birth, with tracking of these alignments continuing throughout one's lifetime.

Atef: A crown consisting of curly ostrich feathers added on either side of the white Hedjet crown.

Atum: Ra-Atum, the setting sun.

Atum-Ra: Ra-Atum, the sun going down.

Aura: A person's energetic field. It surrounds the body as a layer of light. The color of the energy field reflects their state of emotion in the moment.

Ausar: The god of vegetation. He represents the eternal soul. His brother Set cut him into 14 pieces in order to take over the rulership of the kingdom. His wife, Auset, reassembled these pieces and created a golden phallus to replace his missing penis. Even though he was already in spirit form, his reassembled body enabled him to enter the afterlife. From here, he came back in spirit form to father his son Horus.

Auset: The goddess of wisdom and intuition. The wife of Asar who reassembled his lost pieces. Asar came to her in spirit form and impregnated her.

Ba: Crown Chakra, the energy center located at the top of the head.

Baboon: Baboons are the world's largest monkeys. Their outstanding features are their hairless bottoms, long hairless snouts, and hairy heads. They are native to Africa and live in groups that can vary in size from 10 to 300.

Bastet: The cat-shaped goddess who is the protector of households, warding away evil spirits and disease.

Benben stone: The pyramid-shaped part of the obelisk, it represents the stone that was first to arise from the waters of Nun during the process of creation.

Buddhism: A religion with origins in Northern India whose aim is to seek enlightenment within one's self. They believe that spiritual development comes about as a result of an ethical lifestyle.

Byblos: A city in present-day Lebanon.

Canopic Jars: Four jars that housed the stomach, intestines, liver, and lungs and were buried alongside the mummy in the burial tomb. The lids of these jars bore replicas of the gods Hapi, Imsety, Duamutef, and Qebehsenuef in accordance with the bodily organs that each of these gods were in charge of. These gods were collectively called the children of Heru.

Causality, Principle of: This refers to the law of cause and effect. It states that every effect has its cause, and every cause has an effect.

Celtic Religion: A religion with origins in Wales that worships the gods of nature in places like rivers and lakes.

Chakra: The energy centers of the body. Located along the spinal column, they are described as a spinning wheel of light. Each energy center is denoted by a different color.

Christianity: An Abrahamic religion with Jesus Christ as the focal figure.

Correspondence, Principle of: As above, so below. As within, so without. The idea that individual experiences reflect universal experiences. This concept is the basis for the use of astrology to gain insight into an individual's life journey and purpose.

Crown Chakra: The seventh chakra. Located at the top of the head.

Decans: Twelve equal divisions of the year on the Kemetic calendar.

Dendera: A town located west of the Nile at which the Dedera zodiac was found.

Djed: The djed is a pillar made from the tree that grew out of Ausar's coffin when it washed ashore. Ausar was in the coffin after his brother Set tricked him into getting into it before throwing the coffin into a river. The djed represents Ausar's backbone.

Djehuti: The god of the moon, wisdom, intellect, magic, and the written word. He wrote the Emerald Tablets of Thoth.

Djehuti: Thoth, the god of writing and intelligence.

Duamutef: The god who guards the stomach after death.

Duat: The underworld. The place Ra goes to between sunset and sunrise.

Eye of Ra: The team of goddesses sent to implement the law of Ra on earth. The team is made up of Mut, Het-Heru, Bastet, Tefnut, and Nekhbet.

Falcon: A swift and sharp-sighted bird of prey that is capable of hunting other birds by diving at them from above.

Flexitarian: A mostly vegetarian diet with meat consumed in moderation.

Geb: The god of the earth. Twin brother of Nut—goddess of the sky.

Gender, Principle of: Everything has its masculine and feminine aspects.

Hapi: The god who guards the lungs after death.

Hathor: The goddess of the sky. She is in charge of parties and festivals. She encourages gratitude and having fun as a means of life.

Heart Chakra: The fourth chakra. Located in the chest.

Hedjet: The white cone-shaped crown of upper Egypt.

Heka: The god of magic.

Henu: A posture of praise and worship.

Hermes Trismegistus: Hermes three times magnified. Another name for Thoth.

Hermetic: From Hermes Trismegistus.

Hermetic Principles: Universal laws written by Hermes.

Heru: Heru was conceived through a divine union between Auset and the spirit of Ausar. He governs the heart.

Heru-Ur: Horus the elder. The grown-up state of Heru when he was able to fight with his uncle Set and lost his left eye in the process. This left eye, once restored by Thoth, became the wedjat—the eye of Horus. The eye of Horus is also known as the all-seeing eye.

Het-Heru: Hathor, the beautiful goddess of festivities.

Hinduism: A religion from India that follows scriptures known as the Vedas.

Horemakhet: The Sphinx, a man with a lion's body. It represents Horus on the horizon. It is a symbol of the morning sun.

Horus: Heru, the son of Ausar and Auset, who was conceived while Ausarr was in spirit form.

Ibis: A long-legged, long-beaked bird that favors warm weather and marshlands.

Imsety: The god who guards the liver after death.

Initiates: Those on the spiritual journey and possibly on the way to priesthood.

Isis: Auset, the wife of Ausar, who brought him back to life after he was trapped in a coffin and the coffin was thrown into a river.

Islam: An Abrahamic religion based on the teachings of the prophet Muhammad that are inscribed in the Qur'an.

Iusaaset: Grandmother of the gods and goddesses.

Iusas: Iusaaset, the grandmother of divine beings.

Kabbalah: Teachings about Jewish mysticism.

Kemet: The black land, ancient Egypt.

Kemetic: From Kemet.

Khab: Root Chakra, the energy center that is located at the base of the spine.

Khaibit: Sacral Chakra. Located below the belly button.

Khepri: The scarab beetle. It burrows into the mud of the river Nile every year before the annual floods and comes out renewed once the waters have receded.

The rising sun is also Khepri or Ra Khepri, who, having gone into the underworld every night, comes out renewed as the morning sun.

Khu: Third Eye Chakra that is located between your eyebrows and your eyes.

Lotus: A beautiful flower that grows on still water. Also refers to a cross-legged yoga pose.

Ma'at: The goddess of balance and harmony who maintains order in the world. She also weighs the souls of the dead against a feather to determine their suitability to enter the afterlife.

Meditation: Calming the mind and emotions through the

use of focus on an external point or on internal aspects of the self such as the breath.

Mentalism, Principle of: This principle states that the universe is mental due to the supreme consciousness that controls everything from the movement of planets to the behavior of atoms.

Metu Neter: The writings of the gods, hieroglyphics.

Mut: A part of the Eye of Ra, Mut was the wife of Amun-Ra and a mother goddess. She was sometimes depicted as a vulture.

Nbth Hotep: Nebethetepet, a goddess who co-created the world with Ra.

Nebethetepet: The divine feminine co-creator alongside Ra.

Nebthet: Nephthys, the sister of Auset, who disguised herself as her sister and was impregnated by Ausar.

Nefertem: Horus as the divine child of creation. Horus was fathered by spirit and is believed to have existed during and participated in the creation process.

Nehmetawy: Nebethetepet. She helped Ra create the world.

Nephthys: Sister of Auset and goddess of the air.

Neter: The divine force of nature as represented by gods and goddesses who govern the elements.

Nile: The Nile is the biggest river in Egypt. In Kemet, agriculture was focused around this river, depending on its annual flooding to plant seeds into fertile soil for a bountiful harvest.

Ntr: Neter. The gods and goddesses of nature.

Nun: The primordial waters that covered the earth before the creation of land and all living beings.

Nut: The goddess of the night sky and twin sister to Geb, the god of the earth. She is depicted stretched over the earth with the stars painted on her body.

Obelisk: A monolithic pillar with a pyramid at the top. It represents creation and the tree of life. Obelisks channel energy from the atmosphere through their pyramid-shaped tip and dispel it out of their base. In Kemet, obelisks were often made of red granite and placed on either side of the temples. Obelisk heights vary between 10 feet to 100 feet.

Osiris: Ausar, the green god of vegetation and husband to Auset, also known as Isis.

Paleolithic: From the stone age.

Pescatarian: A diet where fish is consumed but red meat and poultry are not consumed.

Pet: The astral plane that houses imagination, dreams, ideas, thoughts, and emotions.

Pharaoh: The name used to refer to the ruler of ancient Egypt. The equivalent of a king.

Polarity, Principle of: Everything has its opposite. Opposites are identical in nature but different in extremes of measurement.

Ptah: The divine blacksmith and the creator of Ra.

Pyramid: This structure has a square base. Each side is triangular-shaped and comes together as a single central point on top. Pyramids are powerful shapes that attract and focus cosmic energy.

Qebehsenuef: The god who guards the intestines after death.

Quantum Physics: The study of the smallest components of physical matter.

Ra: The god of the sun, the creator of the Earth and its inhabitants. He travels across the sky daily from sunrise to sunset.

Ra-Atum: The setting sun.

Ra-Khepri: The rising sun.

Re: Ra, the sun god.

Reiki: An energy healing technique from Japan that uses the hands to impart healing energy to patients.

Rhythm, Principle of: Everything rises and falls; the pendulum swings both ways and in equilibrium.

Root Chakra: The first chakra located at the base of the spine.

Sacral Chakra: The second chakra. Located below the belly button.

Saosis: Iusaaset, grandmother of gods and goddesses who assisted Ra in the creation of the world.

Satet: Set, uncle of Horus and brother to Ausar.

Satis: The goddess of the annual flooding of the Nile River.

Scepter: An ornamental staff with a ball shape at the top.

Sebek: The crocodile god.

Selket: The scorpion goddess.

Sekhem: Life force energy used in energy healing with the use of crystalized rods to direct its power to afflicted areas.

Sekhmet: A lion-headed warrior goddess responsible for bringing pestilence to humankind as retribution for ungodly living. She is also a healer goddess who was worshiped by the priests and priestesses of the healing temples.

Set: God of chaos and confusion who was brother to Asar. He killed his brother for the throne.

Seth: Set, brother of Osiris or Ausar, who tried to kill for the sake of rulership.

Sistrum: A musical instrument that is played in the same way as a tambourine (by shaking it to make the attached disks jingle). It is shaped like an upside-down U, with the bars for the jingles lying horizontally between its two sides.

Shti: The mummy pose, in imitation of the mummy burial pose. When pharaohs were buried, their bodies were preserved through the use of spices and liquids and spices. Thereafter they were wrapped in cloth. The cloth-covered corpse is referred to as a mummy.

Shu: The god of the air.

Solar Plexus Chakra: The third chakra, located above the belly button.

Spirit Guides: Spirits of the dead or of gods and goddesses that work to provide direction to the living.

Ta: The material plane of existence.

Ta-Bitjet: A protective goddess depicted as a scorpion bearing the head of a woman.

Tapping: A method of stress relief that uses acupressure at specific meridian points on the body combined with positive verbal reinforcement.

Tefenet: Tefnut, goddess of moisture and precipitation.

Tefnut: The goddess of (atmospheric) moisture.

Tem Ra: Ra-Atum, the setting sun.

The Assyrians: An ancient civilization emanating from the region of modern-day Iraq, Turkey, Kuwait, and Syria.

The Emerald Tablets of Thoth: Mythical, indestructible green tablets inscribed with knowledge from the sunken world of Atlantis, written by Thoth the Atlantean.

The Mayans: An ancient civilization that existed in the area now covered by Southern Mexico, Guatemala, and Northern Belize.

The Native Americans: The inhabitants of North America before the fifteenth century.

Sahu: Solar Plexus Chakra, located above your belly button.

Shekem: Throat Chakra, located in your throat and denoted with the color blue.

Smai Tawi: Kemetic Yoga, based on hieroglyphics.

Theology: The study of religion.

Theurgy: Consistent actions taken with the aim of attaining divinity by taking on the personality traits of divine beings.

Third Eye Chakra: The sixth chakra, located between the eyes and eyebrows.

Thoth: Djehuti.

Throat Chakra: The fifth chakra. Located in the throat, nose, and thyroid.

Uraeus: The Egyptian cobra. A symbol of divine authority often found depicted on the crowns of pharaohs.

Vegan: A plant-based diet that excludes animal products such as butter, eggs, and milk.

Vegetarian: A plant-based diet.

Vibration, Principle of: Everything vibrates. Nothing is at rest.

Yoga: A method of stretching the body to align body chakras while toning various muscles. Combined with meditation, it enables alignment with the divine.

REFERENCES

AboutBalance (n.d.). Sekhem Energy Healing at About Balance. About Balance. https://www.aboutbalancebrighton.com/sekhem/

Afrikaiswoke (2021). Ancient Kemet's Dendera Zodiac - The world's first zodiac. Afrikaiswoke. https://www.afrikaiswoke.com/ancient-kemets-dendera-zodiac-the-worlds-first-zodiac/

Afrikan History (2022). The Tree Of Life In Ancient Egypt's Metu Neter Explained.AfrikaIsWoke. https://www.afrikaiswoke.com/the-tree-of-life-in-ancient-egypts-metu-neter-explained/

Ahmed, T. (2022). God Serket | Facts Ancient Egyptian Gods and Goddesses | God of fertility, nature, animals, medicine, magic. Hurghada Lovers. https://hurghadalovers.com/god-serket-ancient-egyptian-gods/

Anahana(2022).Chakra Colors. Anahana. https://www.anahana.-com/en/yoga/chakra-colors

Ancient Egypt Wiki (n.d.). Osiris. Ancient Egypt Wiki. https://anciente-gypt.fandom.com/wiki/Osiris

Ancient Egyptian Astrology: Find Your Zodiac Sign (2020). Ancient Egyptian Astrology: Find Your Zodiac Sign. Medium. https://medium.com/la-biblioth%C3%A8que/ancient-egyptian-astrology-find-your-zodiac-sign-c29c705d96ac

AncientEgypt. (n.d.). The 42 Laws And Ideals Of Ma'at. Egypt Connection. https://www.egyptconnection.com/42-laws-of-maat/

Appling, A. (n.d.). Ancient Egyptian Religion. Pinterest. https://pinter-est.com/pin/socalled-martial-arts-never-originated-from-china-or-india-like-others-have-claimed-it-originated-in-africa-and-the-pro--442056519644347127/

Ashby, M. (2002). Kemetic Diet - Ancient African Wisdom For Health of Mind, Body and Spirit. Sema Institute.

Ashby, M. (2008). The Kemetic Tree of Life Ancient Egyptian Metaphysics and Cosmology for Higher Consciousness. Cruzian Mystic Books.

REFERENCES

Ashby. A., Ashby, M. (1997). Egyptian Yoga Movements of the Gods and Goddesses. Cruzian Mystic Books.

Atkinson, W.W. (1908). The Kybalion: A Study of the Hermetic Philosophy of Ancient Egypt and Greece. Yogi Publication Society.

Basubu. (n.d.). 3-Day Egyptian Healing and Meditation Retreat in the Welsh Countryside. Basubu. https://basubu.com/3-day-egyptian-healing-and-meditation-retreat-in-the-welsh-countryside

Below The Stars. (n.d.). Egyptian Astrology: Egyptian Astrology Signs and Their Meanings. Below The Stars. https://belowthestars.com/egyptian-astrology/

Benninghoven, D. (2022). 4 Potential Ways to Increase the pH Level in Your Body. Livestrong. https://www.livestrong.com/article/225555-safest-way-to-raise-body-ph/

Bernard D., Beitman M.D. (2017). I Ching: Intentional Meaningful Coincidences. Psychology Today. https://www.psychologytoday.com/za/blog/connecting-coincidence/201706/i-ching-intentional-meaningful-coincidences?amp

Blanchard, T. (2021). 11 Things That The Tree of Life Represents. Outofstress. https://www.outofstress.com/what-tree-of-life-represents/

Bondy, D. (2020). The Black History of Yoga: A Short Exploration of Kemetic Yoga. Yoga International. https://yogainternational.com/article/view/the-black-history-of-yoga

Bradley, L. (2019). What Is Epigenetics: Your Mind's Influence Over Your Health. SunWarrior. https://sunwarrior.com/blogs/health-hub/epigenetics

Braga, B. (2021). The African Roots Of Kemetic Yoga And How It's Being Adopted By The Diaspora. Travel Noire. https://travelnoire.com/african-root-kemetic-yoga

Braverman, J. (2022). 5 Ways to Remove Acidity From Your Body Naturally. Livestrong. https://www.livestrong.com/article/34910-rid-much-acid-body-naturally/

Brier, B. (2019). Ancient Egyptian Creation Myths: Of Water and Gods. Wondrium Daily. https://www.wondriumdaily.com/ancient-egyptian-creation-myths-of-water-and-gods/

Brier, B. (2020). The Three Gods of Medicine in Ancient Egypt. Wondrium Daily. https://www.wondriumdaily.com/the-three-gods-of-medicine-in-ancient-egypt/

Burgess, L. (2019). What is a paleo diet? Medical News Today. https://www.medicalnewstoday.com/articles/324405#what-is-a-paleo-diet

Canadian Museum Of History. (n.d.). Shu and Tefnut. Canadian Museum Of History. https://www.historymuseum.ca/cmc/exhibitions/civil/egypt/egcrgs4e.html

Chopra, D. (2004). Synchrodestiny: Harnessing the Infinite Power of Coincidence to Create Miraacles. Rider & Co.

Cleopatra Egypt Tours. (2021). Hathor, the Egyptian goddess. Cleopatra Egypt Tours. https://www.cleopatraegypttours.com/travel-guide/hathor-the-egyptian-goddess/

Cleveland Clinic. (2021). How Box Breathing Can Help You Destress - This deep-breathing technique is simple but powerful. Cleveland Clinic. https://health.clevelandclinic.org/box-breathing-benefits/

Colors Explained. (n.d.). Chakra Colors: Guide to 7 Chakras & Their Meanings. Colors Explained. https://www.colorsexplained.com/chakra-colors-and-meanings/

Deif, A. (2008). The Sirius lore. Research Gate. https://www.researchgate.net/publication/267447624_The_Sirius_lore

Deprez, G. (2021). Goddess Isis: Fascinating Facts About The Mother Of All Gods. The Collector. https://www.thecollector.com/ancient-egyptian-goddess-isis/

Discovery World History. (n.d.). Egyptian Healing Rods. Discovery World History. https://discoverywo.blogspot.com/2013/07/egyptian-healing-rods.html?m=1

Dispenza, J. (2021). Plasma, Matter, and the Projection of Reality: Part II. Unlimited. https://drjoedispenza.com/blogs/dr-joes-blog/plasma-matter-and-the-projection-of-reality-part-ii

Education for Life Academy. (2009). World History Timeline. Education For Life Academy. https://educationforlifeacademy.com/world-history-timeline

Egyptian Healing Rods. (n.d.). Science Of Pyramids. Egyptian Healing Rods. https://www.egyptianhealingrods.com/pyramid-research/

Egyptian Healing Rods. (n.d.). Welcome to - Egyptian Healing Rods. Egyptian Healing Rods. https://www.egyptianhealingrods.com/

Egyptian Healing Rods. (n.d.). Russian Research. Egyptian Healing

Rods. https://egyptianhealingrods.me/index_files/EgyptianHealingRod-sRussianResearch.htm

Energy Action. (n.d.). Egyptian Healing Rods – Amplify Your Longevity, Vitality and Intuition. Energy Action. https://energy4action.com/rods-and-pyramids/

Estrada, J. (2021). Each of the 7 Chakras Is Associated With a Color—Here's What Each One Means. Well and Good. https://www.wellandgood.com/chakra-colors-and-meanings/

Fiercely Bright One. (n.d.). Aset FAQ: Frequently Asked Questions about Aset. Fiercely Bright One. https://fiercelybrightone.com/rites/faq-of-aset/

Forti, K. J. (2017). Atlantean Physics Behind Ancient Egyptian Magical Rods. Trifinity 8. https://trinfinity8.com/magic-physics-behind-ancient-egyptian-rods-of-ptah/

Gugliotta, G. (2008). The Great Human Migration - Why humans left their African homeland 80,000 years ago to colonize the world. Smithsonian Magazine. https://www.smithsonianmag.com/history/the-great-human-migration-13561/

Gunnars, K. (2021). 10 Evidence-Based Health Benefits of Intermittent Fasting. Health Line. https://www.healthline.com/nutrition/10-health-benefits-of-intermittent-fasting

Hansen, N.B. (2022). Food in Ancient Egypt: What Did the Egyptians Eat? The Collector. https://www.thecollector.com/food-ancient-egypt/

Hellenic Faith. (n.d.) Theourgia. Hellenic Faith. https://hellenicfaith.com/ritual/

Hill, J. (2016). Shu. Ancient Egypt Online. https://ancientegyptonline.co.uk/shu/

Hill, J. (2009). Kyphi. Ancient Egypt Online https://ancientegyptonline.co.uk/kyphi/

Holland, K. (2022). What Is an Aura? And 15 Other Questions, Answered. Health Line. https://www.healthline.com/health/what-is-an-aura#takeaway

Holmes, K. (2006). Sekhem - A Form of Ancient Egyptian Healing. Positive Health Online. https://www.positivehealth.com/article/reiki/sekhem-a-form-of-ancient-egyptian-healing

IkariusSpirits Healing. (2022). Egyptian Tuning Calibration Healing Rods of Maat - Copper & Zinc - Netu Rods for spiritual calibration and orientation. LinkedIn. https://www.linkedin.com/pulse/egyptian-tuning-calibration-healing-rods-maat-

isidora. (2013). Isis & the Magic of Myrrh. Isiopolis. https://isiopolis.com/2013/07/20/isis-the-magic-of-myrrh/

Isidora. (2022). Of Scorpions, Horus & Isis. Isiopolis. https://isiopolis.com/2022/01/16/of-scorpions-horus-isis/

Jarus, O. (2022). Ancient Egypt: History, dynasties, religion and writing. Live Science. https://www.livescience.com/55578-egyptian-civilization.html

Jayne Leonard, J. (2020). Seven Ways to do Intermittent Fasting. Medical News Today. https://www.medicalnewstoday.com/articles/322293#seven-ways-to-do-intermittent-fasting

Journey To Egypt. (n.d.). Eye of Horus, Eye of Ra. Journey To Egypt. https://www.journeytoegypt.com/en/blog/eye-of-horus

Kalkhurst, J. (2018) My Story With Sekhem-Khrem. Reiki With Jaclyn. https://www.reikiwithjaclyn.com/post/2018/02/22/my-story-with-sekhem-khrem

Kehoe, J. (2011). Quantum Warrior: The Future of the Mind. Zoetic.

Kroll, J. (2017). What Types of Zodiacs Are There Other Than Chinese? Sciencing. https://sciencing.com/types-zodiacs-there-other-chinese-8457677.html

Landious Travel. (n.d.). Goddess Tefnut. Landious Travel. https://landioustravel.com/egypt/egyptian-deities/goddess-tefnut

Landious Travel. (n.d). Nehmetawy goddess. Landious Travel. https://landioustravel.com/egypt/egyptian-deities/nehmetawy-goddess/

LandofKam. (2012). How to Honor Your Ancestors the Kamitic/Kemetic Shaman Way. LandofKam. https://landofkam.wordpress.com/2012/04/28/how-to-honor-your-ancestors-the-kamitic-shaman-way/

Leonard, J. (2019). A guide to EFT tapping. Medical News Today. https://www.medicalnewstoday.com/articles/326434

Lizzy. (2019). Chakra Colors. Chakras.info. https://www.chakras.info/chakra-colors/

Mark, J. J. (2017). Heka. World History Encyclopedia. https://www.worldhistory.org/Heka/

Mark, J. J. (2016). Osiris. World History Encyclopedia. https://www.worldhistory.org/osiris/

Mark, J. J. (2020). The Five Gifts of Hathor: Gratitude in Ancient Egypt. World History Encyclopedia. https://www.worldhistory.org/article/58/the-five-gifts-of-hathor-gratitude-in-ancient-egyp/

Mark, J. J. (2016). Thoth. World History Encyclopedia. https://www.worldhistory.org/Thoth/

Maté, G., Maté, D. (2022). The Myth of Normal: Trauma, Illness, and Healing in a Toxic Culture. Ebury Publishing.

McCammon, E. (2016). Who Is Bastet? Complete Guide to the Egyptian Cat Goddess. PrepScholar. https://blog.prepscholar.com/bastet-egyptian-cat-goddess

McCartney, P. (2021). India's battle against Egypt's Kemetic Yoga. Medium. https://psdmccartney.medium.com/indias-battle-against-egypt-s-kemetic-yoga-6eca5b114d65

McRae, L. (2019). Vegan, Vegetarian, Pescatarian, Flexitarian and Macrobiotic Diets – What's the Difference? North Shore University Health Systems. https://www.northshore.org/healthy-you/vegan-flexitarian-vegetarian-pescatarian-and-macrobiotic-diets--whats-the-difference/

Muhammad, B., Akinyele, P. (2021). Kemetic (Egyptian) Spirituality: The Oldest Faith Tradition. Patch. https://patch.com/new-jersey/newarknj/kemetic-egyptian-spirituality-oldest-faith-tradition

New World Encyclopedia. (n.d.). Ishtar. New World Encyclopedia. https://www.newworldencyclopedia.org/entry/ishtar

Newman, T. (2021). Everything you need to know about Reiki. Medical News Today. https://www.medicalnewstoday.com/articles/308772#summary

Nnaco. (2016). Thoth and The Emerald Tablet. Kanaga. http://www.kanaga.tv/mysticism/toth-and-emerald-tablet.html

Nunez, K . (2020). The Benefits of Breath of Fire and How to Do It. Healthline. https://www.healthline.com/health/breath-of-fire-yoga#safety-tips

Odwirafo. (2017). Hedju ne Antiu Wordpress. https://www.odwirafo.com/Hedju_Antiu.pdf

Oxford Reference. (n.d). Osiris, Killed by Set, Is Resurrected by Isis. Oxford Reference. https://www.oxfordreference.com/display/10.1093/oi/authority.20110803100255831

Oxford University Press. (2018). Nut. Oxford University Press.

https://www.encyclopedia.com/philosophy-and-religion/ancient-religions/ancient-religion/nut-egyptian-goddess

Petre, A. (2018). How to Follow a Raw Vegan Diet: Benefits and Risks. Health Line. https://www.healthline.com/nutrition/raw-vegan-diet#the-diet

Radford, W. (n.d.). Avesa Energy Balancing - Egyptian healing rods and pyramid energy. Radford Holistic Therapies. https://www.radford-holistictherapies.co.uk/avesa_balancing.htm

Realitypathing. (2023). 8 Unique Incense for Ma'at Realitypathing. https://realitypathing.com/8-unique-incense-for-maat/

Regan, S. (2022). Why You Need A Spiritual Bath In Your Life (+ Exactly How To Draw One). MBG Mindfulness. https://www.mind-bodygreen.com/articles/spiritual-bath

Religion Wiki. (n.d.). Iusaaset. Religion Wiki. https://religion.fan-dom.com/wiki/Iusaaset

Rosicrucian Egyptian Museum. (n.d.). Deities in Ancient Egypt - Nephthys. Rosicrucian Egyptian Museum. https://egyptianmuse-um.org/deities-nephthys

Rosicrucian Egyptian Museum. (n.d.). Deities in Ancient Egypt - Seth. https://egyptianmuseum.org/deities-seth

San-Aset. (2022). Iusaaset, Goddess of the Tree of Life. IsemSanctuary. https://iseumsanctuary.com/2022/02/14/goddess-of-the-tree-of-life/

Scaccetti, J. (n.d.). The connection between chakra blockages and emotional and physical conditions. Agent Nateur. https://www.agentna-teur.com/blogs/agent-tips/p-strong-the-connection-between-chakra-blockages-and-emotional-and-physical-conditions-strong-p-p-p?utm_source=google&utm_medium=paid&utm_cam-paign=17683018728&utm_content=&utm_term=&gadid=&gclid=EA-IaIQobChMIsp2z57ba-wIVjLHtChorqQTXEAAYAiAAEgKWavD_BwE

Scher, A. B. (n.d.). 7 Ridiculously Simple Tapping Techniques To Unblock Your Chakras. Soul & Spirit. https://www.soulandspirit-magazine.com/13951-2/

Shane Clayton. (2022). The Sacred Temple Incense of Ancient Egypt. Wandering Stars https://www.wandering-stars.net/kepu-temple-incense

Shane Clayton. (2022). The Seven Sacred Oils. Pomegranate Flounder

REFERENCES

https://pomegranate-flounder-c98k.squarespace.com/the-seven-sacred-oils

Shetty, J. (2020). 20 Days of Live Meditation with Jay Shetty: Day 1. YouTube. https://youtu.be/gxURcDSeRns

Shridhar, G., Rajendra, N., Murigendra, H. (2015). Modern Diet and its Impact on Human Health. Journal of Nutrition & Food Sciences. https://www.longdom.org/open-access/modern-diet-and-its-impact-on-human-health-35026.html

Solarnayoga. (n.d.). The Rods Of The Egyptians. Solarnayoga. https://solarnayoga.info/pdf/Egyptians_Rods_or_Wands_of_Horus.pdf

Sound And Light. (n.d.). 10 Interesting Facts about Hathor; goddess of motherhood. Sound And Light. https://soundand-light.show/en/blog/10-interesting-facts-about-hathor

Stanford Medicine. (n.d.). Anatomy and Function of the Liver. Stanford Medicine. https://www.stanfordchildrens.org/en/topic/default?id=anatomy-and-function-of-the-liver-90-P03069

Stanton, KM. (2022). Tree of Life Meaning, Symbolism, and Mythology. UniGuide. https://www.uniguide.com/tree-of-life

Stuetz , T.T. (2010). Healing Secrets of the Pharaohs-Egyptian Healing Rods. Ezine Articles. https://ezinearticles.com/?Healing-Secrets-of-the-Pharaohs-Egyptian-Healing-Rods&id=4914300

svarthaxan. (2021). Anubis as my spirit guide. Reddit. https://www.reddit.com/r/Kemetic/comments/l1xolf/anubis_as_my_spirit_guide/

Swan Bazaar. (2021). The Four Sons of Horus. Swan Bazaar. https://www.swanbazaar.com/Blog/post/the-four-sons-of-horus

Swan Bazaar. (2021). The Four Sons of Horus. Swan Bazaar. https://www.swanbazaar.com/Blog/post/the-four-sons-of-horus

templeofathena. (2011). Offerings for Anubis Wordpress. https://templeofathena.wordpress.com/2011/02/17/offerings-for-anubis/

Tewari, A. (2022). 700 Affirmations to Balance All 7 Chakras. Gratefulness Blog. Https://blog.gratefulness.me/chakra-affirmations/amp/

The Earth Center. (n.d.). The Kemetic Meso-American Connection. The Earth Center. https://www.theearthcenter.org/post/in-search-of-the-gods-the-kemetic-meso-american-connection

The Editors of Encyclopaedia Britannica(n.d.). 11 Egyptian Gods and

Goddesses. Encyclopaedia Britannica. https://www.britannica.-com/list/11-egyptian-gods-and-goddesses

The Editors of Encyclopaedia Britannica. (n.d.). Horus - Egyptian god. Encyclopaedia Britannica. https://www.britannica.com/topic/Horus

The Gut-Brain Connection: How it Works and The Role of Nutrition. (2020). The Gut-Brain Connection: How it Works and The Role of Nutrition. Health Line. https://www.healthline.com/nutrition/gut-brain-connection#TOC_TITLE_HDR_5

Toliver, A. (n.d.). Greatest Story Ever Stolen - An exploration of the stolen legacy of Kush, Kemet, and all world religions. Sutori. https://www.sutori.com/en/story/greatest-story-ever-stolen--UamyoBPaDaVejpn775pZxCrH

Urban Wellness Hub. (n.d.). Egyptian Sekhem. Urban Wellness Hub. https://www.urbanwellnesshub.co.uk/egyptian-sekhem

Vampire Rave. (2021). Egyptian Chakras & Energetics. Vampire Rave. https://www.vampirerave.com/houses/house_page.php?house=python&page=18012

Vigne, L. (2019). The 42 ideals of Ma'at. Kemet Experience. https://www.kemetexperience.com/the-42-ideals-of-maat/

Young, S.P. (2019). Nine Parts of the Human Soul According to the Ancient Egyptians. Ancient Origins. https://www.ancient-origins.net/human-origins-religions/ancient-egyptian-soul-0012390

YOUR FEEDBACK IS VALUED

We would like to be so bold as to ask for an act of kindness from you. If you read and enjoyed our book/s, would you please consider leaving an honest review on Amazon or audible? As an independent publishing group, your feedback means the absolute world to us. We read every single review we receive and would love to hear your thoughts, as each piece of feedback helps us serve you better. Your feedback may also impact others across the globe, helping them discover powerful knowledge they can implement in their lives to give them hope and self-empowerment. Wishing you empowerment, courage, and wisdom on your journey.

If you have read or listened to any of our books and would be so kind as to review them, you can do so by clicking the 'learn more' tab under the book's picture on our website:

https://ascendingvibrations.net/books

Why not join our Facebook community and discuss your spiritual path with like-minded seekers?

We would love to hear from you!

Go here to join the 'Ascending Vibrations' community:

bit.ly/ascendingvibrations